FOOTBALLEUR

Robert Pires
with Xavier Rivoire

Translated by Dominic Fifield

YELLOW JERSEY PRESS

LONDON

Published by Yellow Jersey Press 2003

10 9

Copyright © Robert Pires 2002

Translation copyright © Dominic Fifield 2003

Robert Pires has asserted his right under the Copyright, Designs and Patents Act 1988 to be identified as the author of this work

First published in Great Britain in 2003 by
Yellow Jersey Press

Yellow Jersey Press
Random House, 20 Vauxhall Bridge Road,
London SW1V 2SA

Random House Australia (Pty) Limited
20 Alfred Street, Milsons Point, Sydney,
New South Wales 2061, Australia

Random House New Zealand Limited
18 Poland Road, Glenfield,
Auckland 10, New Zealand

Random House (Pty) Limited
Endulini, 5A Jubilee Road, Parktown 2193,
South Africa

The Random House Group Limited Reg. No. 954009
www.randomhouse.co.uk

A CIP catalogue record for this book
is available from the British Library

ISBN 0-224-06980-2

Papers used by Random House are natural, recyclable products made from wood grown in sustainable forests. The manufacturing processes conform to the environmental regulations of the country of origin

Typeset by SX Composing DTP, Rayleigh, Essex
Printed and bound in Great Britain by
Mackays of Chatham plc, Chatham, Kent

Contents

List of Illustrations

Foreword

Robert Pires had just jogged off the training pitch, sharing a joke with Thierry Henry en route and oblivious to the ugly scar etched across his right knee, when Arsène Wenger announced to the waiting media that his French talisman was ready to return. 'He brings vision, he has a great work-rate and a special passing ability,' said the Arsenal manager to a chorus of short-hand scribbling in the dining room at London Colney. 'We are more fluent with him on the pitch. He is the oil in our engine.'

Wenger is not one for fanfares, but the Double-winning manager trumpeted this comeback from the rafters. It was six months to the day since Pires had jumped to avoid the Newcastle defender Nicos Dabizas's innocuous challenge, landing awkwardly on the touchline as the ball squirmed away, and, with his leg buckling under him, heard the agonising crack. The anterior cruciate ligament in his right knee had ruptured; a career that had been touching greatness was suddenly thrown into doubt. The Premiership run-in, the pursuit of the FA Cup, even the summer's

defence of the World Cup in South Korea and Japan . . .
any hopes the French international had of ending a dazzling
second season at Highbury with the bang it deserved had
been wrecked.

So began months of morale-sapping, painstaking recovery,
weeks of unbearable frustration spent teaching his body
how to function again almost from scratch, its robotics
disrupted by the trauma in his right leg. And always there
was nagging self-doubt. Would he return the same player?
The man who had inspired Arsenal's slick, irresistible
challenge during the 2001/02 season, who had become as
much a fulcrum for the France manager Roger Lemerre as
the apparently peerless Zinedine Zidane? Pires's grinning
entrance into the London Colney dressing rooms that
October afternoon in 2002 suggested those six months of
intense emotions were indeed behind him. The knee had
been reconstructed, its rehabilitation undertaken in France,
Wenger's daily phone calls and regular pep-talks maintaining the 29-year-old's motivation.

Some 36 hours after his manager's endorsement, and
with his side trailing Auxerre 2–0, Pires was summoned
from his warm-up jogs up and down the touchline. Highbury had been hollering all evening for his introduction, the
home partisans' clamour exacerbated by the sight of their
favourites inexplicably down by two goals, and with 19
minutes remaining their pleas were answered. Up went the
board – 19 7 – off trotted the Brazilian Gilberto Silva and,
to the din of a delirious welcome, on came D'Artagnan.

In truth, his performance that night was more frenetic

than focused, all adrenalin-charged enthusiasm with little
shape or pattern, and Arsenal duly lost 2–1. It was their
second successive defeat, three days after the club's first loss
in 31 League games, at Goodison Park, from where the
news of Wayne Rooney's stunning late winner was relayed
by text message to a flabbergasted Pires, who was recovering from a reserve-team game against Queens Park Rangers
('I was rubbish' was his assessment of that display).
Mystifyingly, two more reverses quickly followed: a sloppy
2–1 home defeat at the hands of Blackburn and a
Champions League débâcle in Dortmund. Arsenal's worst
sequence of results in 19 years was hardly a fitting way to
welcome back the Footballer of the Year.

Yet, for Pires, the green shoots of progress were there:
glimpses of his trademark shimmying and serene running
style, his gliding across the turf, his caressing of the ball in
the pass, his creeping back into the midfielders' play. Each
game showed an improvement, a stiffening of a fragile
confidence, the stunning shot that exploded beyond Jurgen
Macho into the net during the 3–2 Worthington Cup
defeat to Sunderland in early November confirming as
much. The North Bank breathed again.

Great players have struggled to overcome similarly
serious injuries – Paul Gascoigne was never the same after
his self-inflicted ligament rupture in the 1991 FA Cup final;
Alan Shearer has never been able to boast the pace of old
since breaking his leg in 1997 – but the Frenchman was
following the lead set by Ronaldo and Ruud van
Nistelrooy. The sight of the Brazilian marksman back to his

best in Japan, propelling his country towards dislodging France as world champions, provided a fillip; after his knee troubles, the Dutchman's prodigious first season terrorising English club defences with United, even in Arsenal's slipstream, had done the same.

At least the uncomfortable feeling of trailing slightly off the pace was nothing new for Pires, and, significantly, it had been overcome before. The gummy form was merely a throwback to the toil he had endured during his first six months in north London two years earlier when the flailing arms and fearsome tackling of the English game nullified the impact of the £6m signing from Marseille. Named as a substitute for his first Premier League game back in August 2000, Pires had watched aghast from the dug-out as Sunderland's rugged campaigners flung themselves at Arsenal as if they were barbarians in a Ridley Scott movie. For Pires, wide-eyed and as much disturbed as excited by what he had witnessed, it was a baptism of fire.

By Christmas the championship was as good as surrendered to Manchester United, and as Arsenal trailed in their wake the suggestion remained that Wenger's big-money gamble – a fortune spent on a bit-part World Cup winner who had, it was argued, struggled and lost the captaincy at Marseille, another big underachieving club – had failed spectacularly. There was tutting on the terraces. 'Not strong enough,' came the grumbles; 'Not up to it . . . the game's too physical for him.'

But Wenger is a better judge than that, and Pires a better player. In his second season the change was staggering: the distinctive swashbuckling sprints, the graceful and incisive passing, and the sublime flicks and spins were unrecognisable from the rather tentative probing that had characterised his first year at Highbury. Full-backs shrank away at the sight of the Frenchman, hair flowing as he tore at them to cross waspishly or cut inside and leave his marker a blubbering wreck on the turf.

There were goals, too, taken with increasing aplomb, from the stunning to the simple. At Villa Park, in a game Arsenal were struggling to close down, Pires took the breath away with a strike of such stunning beauty, such outrageous impudence, as to prompt mathematicians to peer incredulously at their protractors, perplexed by the trajectory the midfielder had conjured to chip the giant Peter Schmeichel from unfeasibly close in.

Six days later, Pires lay crumpled and broken on the Highbury turf, clutching his right knee in agony. The game was up. Arsenal might have responded in suitably breathtaking fashion – the next eight Premiership games won, the title claimed gloriously and aptly at Old Trafford within a few days of victory over Chelsea in the FA Cup final in Cardiff – but the repercussions of the Frenchman's loss thundered across the Channel. Lemerre, who had picked the former Metz midfielder as the left-prong of a trident midfield behind a lone striker in all his internationals since France had won Euro 2000, described the news as 'devastating'. 'I think it will also affect the whole of France,' he growled in Clairefontaine.

Yet now, with his country relieved of their world crown

and Arsenal desperate to continue their domestic domin-
ance, Pires is back. 'It is a challenge for me to try to return
to my best, and, to be honest, there's so much more hard
work to be done,' he admitted after playing the final 20
minutes of the 1–0 Premiership win over Newcastle in
November. There was a neat symmetry to that result: a
return fixture with the Geordies, against whom he had
suffered his injury, with Arsenal back to winning ways and
their French talisman re-established in the fold after six
months out.

This book details that journey from treatment room back
to the first team, as well as Pires's own development from
rookie wannabe to international star. It examines the strains,
both on and off the pitch, of life as a professional footballer,
from his grounding at Stade de Reims through a turbulent
spell at Marseille to his arrival in the big-time of the
Premiership. At the time of going to press, Pires admits he
does not know how long his latest journey, his ongoing
attempt to return to the blistering form of 2001/02, will
take. He does not even know whether it is realistic to
expect such a thing at all. 'People will have to be patient,
but I'm looking at it as exciting,' he says. 'I have nothing to
lose. I can only improve.'

Dominic Fifield
November 2002

FOOTBALLEUR

1

A Knackered Knee

I'll always remember the sound of my name being chanted to the rafters as I discarded my crutches by the touchline, limped out on to the pitch and mounted the podium. I was the last of the players to hold the Premiership trophy aloft and, as I raised it above my head, my team-mates standing below me on the Highbury turf bowed down. Patrick Vieira, Thierry Henry, David Seaman, Tony Adams . . . the noise from the stands was deafening, but it was the sight of these great players pretending to worship me that sent a shiver down my spine. To have played a part in helping this Arsenal side claim the Double in May 2002 was an honour, but to receive such an ovation from the crowd and such adulation from my team-mates – even if it was tongue in cheek – was something else. That sums up the spirit at this club.

Back then my knee was still in a brace as I steadily continued my recovery from the surgery I had undergone two months earlier. That brief, joyous return to Highbury was the last time I saw a lot of the lads until I pulled on an

Arsenal shirt again at the pre-season photocall in mid-August. We met up at the club's London Colney training centre, it was wonderful to see them all, and for the first time in five months I kicked a ball with my team-mates. But being there with them all and then having to watch from the sidelines, kicking my heels and unable to take part in training, was too hard. I returned to France, my determination renewed to be back fully fit and playing again with the Gunners as soon as possible. I'm at home at Highbury, and the next time we celebrate a Double I'll be there without my crutches.

★

23 March 2002: Arsenal had the Premiership title and the FA Cup within sight, I was enjoying my best form for the club and everything was looking up. In the League we'd just established ourselves at the top of the table by beating Aston Villa 2–1 at Villa Park with my ninth Premiership goal of the season helping to seal the victory. We were also close to an FA Cup semi-final place. At the beginning of March we'd not been able to finish off Newcastle on Tyneside, the quarter-final finishing in a tantalising 1–1 draw. The replay was back at Highbury and the build-up was the same as ever. We met at the ground on the Friday evening before the game and travelled by bus to a hotel for the night. This was to be my 45th game of the season for Arsenal and I did feel a bit tired, but I was still looking forward to the match.

The game was due to kick off at midday on the Saturday. I must say I'm not a big fan of matches being brought forward for television. Footballers are more suited to playing either in the afternoon or early evening – that's what you're used to. All right, an earlier kick-off allows the fans to go to the match and then have the rest of the day free, and of course television gets to show the game at prime time. But I always feel as if I'm not quite awake in matches like these.

Having said that, it didn't take me long to get into the swing of things against Newcastle. Two minutes in, I picked up the ball just to the left of United's penalty area in one of our first attacks. There was no time to control the pass, I just shot first time and it beat Shay Given's dive for my 13th goal of the season in all competitions. Thirteen. I'm not superstitious but maybe that should have crossed my mind, though I was too lost in the adrenalin-pumped occasion. At around the 15-minute mark I crossed from the left for Dennis Bergkamp, loitering at the far post, who duly put us two up and as good as through.

Then it happened. Freddie Ljungberg chased a long ball and competed for possession with Nicos Dabizas. Arriving to help him out, I had to vault the Greek defender's tackle down on the goal-line; as I landed on my right leg, my foot got stuck in the turf and my knee buckled under me.

These days, I'll shy away from watching re-runs of the incident on the telly. Every time I've seen it it's made me feel sick. I remember hearing the crack and feeling a familiar tearing sensation in my knee. While playing for Metz about five years previously I'd had the same experience. On that occasion I was out for a month, my cruciate ligament badly damaged but not ruptured. At Highbury, as I was carried from the pitch to the changing rooms on a stretcher, the memory of that injury replayed in my mind.

But at first it didn't seem too bad. At half-time I could even stand up. My team-mates came to see how I was and I told Thierry Henry, who was suspended and watching the game from the stands, that it was just a bad strain. I told myself I'd be out for two to four weeks at most, that's all. I was mentally prepared for the club doctor to say as much. There was still hope.

There were tests, consultations, X-rays and MRI scans – I'd been injured before and I knew the drill well enough. And then the verdict came: I'd ruptured the anterior cruciate ligament in my right knee and would be out for six months. I'd been prepared for and had even accepted the fact that I would miss the build-up to the World Cup with the French national team, but now I was being told that I wouldn't make the tournament itself. It would be the longest period I'd ever been out of the game, with nothing but a slim hope of being fit for the start of the next season. I felt utterly demoralised.

Injuries always come along and floor you when you least expect them but, if only in hindsight, there's always some physical or psychological explanation as to why they happen. This one came about because I had been careless. Maybe I was mentally fatigued, I told myself. Yes, that was it. I just wasn't concentrating. I must have been worn out by the endless run of games, the constant competition. That was enough to make me land awkwardly and wreck my knee. For injury, read tiredness.

Between August 2001 and March 2002 I had played 45 games for Arsenal – 28 in the Premiership, 12 in the Champions League and five in the cups – as well as having lined up five times for France. Those selections had often taken me around the globe; long-haul flights and games in places like Australia and Chile take their toll, with club matches adding up at home as well. The football calendar in England is without doubt the most demanding in the world. But when you sign up to play for Arsenal, you know what you're letting yourself in for. There are more games in England, that's just the way it is.

As a professional sportsman I don't agree with drug use to enhance performance, but the fixture list in football today shows no mercy and the need always to be at the top of your game explains why that problem exists. My education, gleaned both from my parents and as a young footballer at Reims and Metz, taught me never to regard illegal stimulants as the solution to a problem. As a top-level sportsman, if you are struggling to compete it's because you are tired and you just have to accept it. It's part of the game. It can be infuriating, demoralising and very stressful, but when your body tells you it's feeling the pace you can't just cheat your opponent and turn to stimulants. That's not the answer, and in my opinion any footballer who resorts to drugs should be penalised without hesitation. And the only way to discourage abuse is anti-dope testing, which is an integral part of sport and should remain so.

On the other hand, as professionals, all we can do about the ridiculous number of games we have to play is to keep

publicly repeating: 'We play a lot, probably too much.'
Every time we bang on about it it sounds as if we're
whingeing, particularly given the salaries top-flight
footballers command these days, but that's missing the
point. Look at how England and, more pertinently, France
fared at the 2002 World Cup – those players were clearly
exhausted because they'd been overplayed by their clubs.
Common sense should kick in at some stage, surely.

Don't get me wrong. I'm always happy to be picked and
my injury hasn't changed the way I think, but it would
seem sensible to shorten the domestic season. Why not
reduce the number of teams in the English top flight from
20 to 18, like in France? That would be a way of cutting
back on the number of Premiership games. Similarly, you
could rearrange the international calendar. I'm thinking
about the European Championship qualifying games for
2004: why didn't UEFA make those countries outside their
top 20 pre-qualify before the bigger countries entered the
competition? That would have made sense.

I now had to face up to the pain, both physical and
mental, of my injury. When I felt my right knee crack I
instinctively crumpled, grimacing, to the turf with my
thumb pushed in where the ligament had ruptured. By
digging my thumb in at that spot it helped block out the
pain and dampen the initial shock of the injury.

Every footballer knows pain is part and parcel of life as
a professional athlete. It's part of the job; at some stage,
you're bound to be struck down by injury. The possibility
that you might rupture knee ligaments – the bones,

muscles and tendons in the joint make it one of the most complex parts of the human body – haunts footballers, but when it actually happened to me I wasn't thinking about what it might mean in the long-term. There was only room in my head for the pain. It was so intense and all-consuming. I hardly slept at all the night after the injury. I couldn't bend my knee and the pain built up and seemed to spread through every joint. My whole body seemed to throb with mind-numbing pain. Over my career I hadn't done my knee any favours and it sure as hell wasn't going to do any for me now.

For anyone, pain can be as much to do with the psychological as the physical. But for footballers it's worse. Injuries prompt frustration, disillusionment and ultimately a real loss of motivation. This can be helped with therapy, but for some the damage is irreparable and I was determined not to be one of those, not to let it get the better of me. You do eventually come to know what kind of injury provokes what kind of pain, but it's a tough learning curve and you make mistakes from time to time, just as I had done with my hopeful prognosis on my knee.

I was better prepared than most, though, to deal with the situation. As a recently turned professional at Metz I was put through brutally strenuous training sessions that were designed to build up my endurance, and as a result I came to see pain as being part of everyday life. It was part of getting back to full fitness and well-being in pre-season; you had to master it, limit it, get used to it and integrate it into your thinking. It was the same with injuries. Treat the initial pain as well and as quickly as possible, but then accept it and get on with your life. I had to live with this damaged right knee. But then I had never suffered a serious injury before; this was going to be a new type of struggle.

The day after the Newcastle game I had to consult specialists to ascertain what to do next. The two experts I saw offered two completely different plans of action, leaving me with a choice: should I undergo an operation or not? No one else could make the decision. It would be up to me alone, though when it came to it there was plenty of interference from all sides, with a lot of advice aired unadvisedly in public. Too many doctors can spoil the patient.

The following Sunday I underwent an MRI scan to detect the lesions on the tissue and ligaments that ordinary X-rays can't pick up. I was in the hands of Philippe Boixel, the Arsenal chiropractor and osteopath who also works with the French national team. Then, the next day, when I should have been with the French squad who were meeting up to prepare for a friendly against Scotland, I was instead in a car heading for Strasbourg to consult Dr Jean-Henri Jaeger. The France coach Roger Lemerre had instructed me to make the trip, but Arsène Wenger sorted it all out and contacted the surgeon himself.

Dr Jaeger, one of the most respected knee specialists in the world, examined me. I remember the way he poked and prodded the leg, then looked up and said soberly, 'It'll be six months, but we'll need to operate.' Six months? So that was it. My World Cup was over even before it had begun. The reality was that I would not be playing any part in the 2002 tournament. The news was hard to take and hurt me almost as badly as the injury.

Time, from the moment the doctor uttered his prognosis to the point when I faced the press and my team-mates back in Paris, just washed over me. I was in shock. I travelled back to the capital where a chauffeur-driven car was waiting for me. I was then taken to Clairefontaine, just outside Paris and the home of *Les Bleus*, where I would have to greet my colleagues and face the public. I sat in the back of the car, feeling numb. All I could think about was the World Cup, the dream of every little boy who's ever kicked a football. France was to defend the glorious victory of 1998 with a group of players that was, in my opinion, stronger and more confident than ever before. This tournament was going to be the culmination of years of hard work and careful planning for the national squad. And now I was going to miss out. That was a bitter pill to swallow.

I tried to think of the positive things. I was only 28 and I might still have a chance of playing in the next World Cup in 2006. That should be my objective. I had other things to look forward to as well, not just with my club or my country, but in life outside football. There was plenty I could achieve before the tournament began in Germany in four years' time.

Sitting in the back of the car, winding its way slowly through Paris, I also thought about the people who really counted in my professional and personal lives. I pictured their faces, I relived the moments that had fashioned my career. It was as if I had died and was rewinding through the key moments of my life – this stream of memories, of dates and games passed through my head. It wasn't as if I was daydreaming; I felt genuinely lucky. I thought of those people in hospitals or on the streets who hadn't had the good fortune I'd had, and slowly I put everything into perspective. By the time I reached Clairefontaine I had accepted my lot. Life wasn't that bad after all.

Yet on my arrival the looks on some of my team-mates' faces suggested they were the ones facing long-term injury, not me. They looked dejected, and the sight of me with a big smile was clearly a bit disconcerting for them all. They didn't understand, but it wasn't that I was making light of my situation or the real honour I feel whenever I'm selected for the national team, I just wasn't going to make a point of feeling sorry for myself. I knew this French team and I was convinced – wrongly, as it turned out – that it was going to do well with or without me in South Korea and Japan. If I'd arrived in tears, banging on about how I shouldn't have had to jump a tackle or even play against Newcastle, what good would it have done? After all, if you really love playing so much, it shouldn't be a chore actually to get out there and practise your chosen profession. And, of course, we are paid for the privilege.

A lot of people were affected by my injury, but amid all the fuss that was being made of my situation I managed to continue to put the blow into perspective. I called upon my experiences at Marseille where I'd occasionally gone to visit patients in the local hospitals. I saw ten-year-old youngsters who couldn't walk, so why should I feel sorry for myself? I

was only going to be out for six months. The only thing that
got on my nerves was to hear some people saying I'd feigned
serious injury to give me some time off before the World
Cup. They didn't know what they were talking about and
must have felt pretty foolish to see the MRI scans proved
right and me on the sidelines for such a long time.

What I wanted to focus on was getting back to the level
I had been at before the injury. I'd been enjoying the form
of my life at Arsenal, and as I sat on a bench on the edge of
the pitch watching my French colleagues I just wanted to
look forward to a time when I was fully fit and could
contribute in a meaningful way to my national side too. I
stayed with the team that Monday evening, my presence
reminding them that they had to be careful for the rest of
the season and guard against injuries like mine. Many of the
team were playing prominent roles in their respective
domestic championships. Some of us were still involved in
the latter stages of the Champions League. I was a stark
reminder of what could happen to any of them at any time.
But I remember the atmosphere that evening as positive.
My smiles over supper were not for the cameras; it felt good
to be there with them all.

Dr Jaeger had advised me to have the operation as soon
as possible, but before I made any rash decisions I wanted to
get a second opinion and turned for advice to another
respected surgeon, Dr Franceschi in Marseille. After all, the
last thing I needed at that stage was a 'knee-jerk' reaction.
On the Tuesday morning he examined the knee and
confirmed the ruptured ligament, but, unlike Dr Jaeger, he

was less convinced about the need to operate. Instead, he thought I should take three weeks to rest and then have another examination before going under the knife. At the same time, the French team doctor Jean-Marcel Ferret, basically passing on a message from Roger Lemerre to the outside world, let it be known publicly that I had a 10 to 15 per cent chance of avoiding surgery. Surprise surprise, his comments were immediately translated in the press as 'Pires has a 10 to 15 per cent chance of making the World Cup', suggesting that if I opted to allow the ligament to heal naturally rather than undergo the surgery, a miracle may yet happen. The debate raged in the newspapers, quoting Drs Jaeger and Saillant (another world-renowned knee specialist) recommending the operation and Dr Ferret suggesting otherwise. I just wanted to be left alone.

I had in fact already made my decision to take the three weeks and let things calm down. I kept my own counsel while all around me people I had consulted were mouthing off about a decision that was down to me and me alone. Medical matters are supposed to be private and it was a disgrace that anyone felt the need to talk about the matter publicly. I may be a footballer playing for my country, but that doesn't mean I should have to share my medical notes with the press and the people of France. Especially as I'm a sportsman and my body is effectively the tool of my trade. It was my health and my career that was at stake, no one else's. My livelihood was on the line. But, for the press, a story's a story, and when it comes to football there's nothing that's out of bounds.

It would all have been so different if I'd left the doctors'
surgeries, summoned the press and bellowed to anyone who
wanted to listen, 'Well, I've just come out of an
examination with Dr Jaeger and he has told me this and
that, and stressed this and that. And I've also seen Dr
Franceschi and this is what he told me . . .' In his defence,
Jean-Marcel Ferret was badgered slightly by the media
having attended two press conferences at the French camp
at which questions were hurled at him from all sides. But as
far as Jean-Henri Jaeger is concerned, he seemed only too
eager to talk publicly on the matter. Even so, I don't hold
it against him, though I doubt I'll be rushing to consult him
again in the future. A sportsman coming to terms with an
injury needs a period of calm just to take stock and weigh
up his options. In my case, the week after I damaged my
knee was a media circus, a noisy public debate about things
that should have remained private. I felt badly let down.

On the Friday after France's 5–0 victory over Scotland, a
game I watched from the stands, I returned to Arsenal's
training ground at London Colney to meet with Arsène
Wenger and the club's medical staff. We agreed on the
diagnosis that had been made from the MRI scan – I
definitely had a rupture of the anterior ligament of my right
knee – and on the necessary treatment. We were going to
wait three weeks for the swelling in the knee to go down
then, depending on the state of the joint, we'd either pursue
a gentle rehabilitation if it appeared the ligament could heal
itself (as advocated by Dr Ferret) or we'd go ahead with the
surgery Dr Jaeger had advised. We just wanted to get the

knee back to normal as best we could, and Arsène would back me in whatever decision I took, even if he was desperate to have me back in contention and playing at the start of the 2002/03 season.

So my rehabilitation began. Your club or national team can arrange for you to consult various specialists, but it's always up to the player to decide which surgeon or physio actually sees you through. I chose Philippe Boixel, and he went to Arsène and recommended I spend a fortnight at his clinic in France to try to ease the bruising around my knee. Philippe also works for the best clubs across Europe, including the likes of Juventus and Parma, and as soon as I arrived at his office in Laval I felt as if I was in the hands of real experts.

Most Arsenal fans wouldn't know the name Philippe Boixel, but the players recognise he has a pivotal role to play behind the scenes. Matches take a physical toll, the body takes a lot of punishment, and the manager calls on his osteopath whenever someone's limping or tired or aching. He gets us back on our feet, targeting the areas that are knotted up or under stress, manipulating the internal workings of the body and then using massage to get the blood flowing again. It's like yoga, though osteopathy is a medical discipline in its own right.

Everyone's body is different and an individual's ailments are a result of how he jumps, lands and runs, and what strains, bruising or cramps each body is particularly susceptible to. Boixel is a body mechanic, and his years of experience have taught him how to diagnose and recognise

what treatment is best suited to relieve each player's aches
and pains. Osteopathy and physiotherapy complement each
other, but they are distinct disciplines. Philippe Boixel and
his team used their combined skills to work on the whole
of my leg rather than just my knee.

At the beginning of April I left for a fortnight in Laval. I
stayed in a hotel and spent every day in Boixel's surgery,
with Arsenal picking up the bill. I had been injured playing
for them and was covered by the medical insurance that the
club takes out on all its players. Financially, I would have
been ready to pay up if there had been a problem with the
insurance; after all, I was still receiving my salary while I was
sidelined, like any injured footballer under contract.

I spent all day on the treatment table. The treatment was
seriously intensive. There were sessions in the morning, the
afternoon and in the evening with an hour and a half's
break for lunch. At the end of the day I would return to my
hotel room more knackered than I would normally be
during the season when I was playing. Mickael Verron, the
physio based at Philippe Boixel's surgery, looked after me
most of the time. He massaged me and drained the fluids
around my damaged right knee until the bruising had
receded. The idea was to bring the swelling down and to try
to restore some of the usual movement, always with the
operation in mind.

But it wasn't just a matter of massaging the muscles in the
one leg. When you suffer an injury like this, you not only
have to work on the area that is damaged but also maintain
physical work on the whole body so you don't lose strength

elsewhere. I was working as much on the good left leg as the right, lifting weights tied to my ankle while at the same time the physio steadily improved my right leg, which I could now bend, albeit slowly. I kept hoping that I wouldn't have to have an operation and that I might even be out for only three months rather than six. It was tempting to be that optimistic, every day hoping that the next MRI scan would show positive signs, but I was kidding myself.

It helped me to think about people like Thomas Castaignède, the French rugby player who plays for Saracens. My injury was nothing compared to his. It was two years since he'd ruptured his Achilles tendon and he was still not fully fit. There'd been complications on the grafts he'd had on the injury and he'd only recently started running again. Imagine the body as a Formula One racing car – if one part breaks down, the rest of the machine starts misfiring. Thomas not only had to rehabilitate the tendon, but also the calf and his ankle. The intricacies of the ligaments and muscles are complex and it's hard to get the area around the tendon to heal properly. The same thing happened to Florian Maurice, the former Olympique Lyonnais, Paris Saint-Germain and Olympique de Marseille striker. He's back playing and scoring again now, having done well on loan in Spain with Celta Vigo and more recently with Bastia, but he'd suffered several relapses and had ended up sidelined for ages. But I kept trying to reassure myself. At least with a knee ligament injury, a relatively common problem for footballers, I had a chance. It could have been a lot worse.

When I first arrived in London Thierry Henry introduced me to Thomas Castaignède and I spent quite a lot of time with him. We became friends, sharing our mutual problems. We still talk about the injuries now. He phoned me recently, saying, 'Hi there, could I speak to Crock Number Two, please?'

'Who's calling?'

'It's Crock Number One.'

'All right, if it's another cripple then we can talk.'

'In that case, how is the most valuable knee in the world doing?'

It helps having another sportsman to talk to and share experiences with during your recuperation, but it also helped me to see fellow professionals who had fully recovered from their injuries, like Ronaldo who'd been sidelined for two years, or Ruud van Nistelrooy at Manchester United. They'd both returned and were back at their best, scoring goals at club and international level, and that gave me hope. Look at what Ronaldo achieved during the 2002 World Cup.

However, all that was a long way off. I wasn't prepared for the length of time I would spend on the treatment table. At the beginning of my rehabilitation I found myself completely exhausted, overwhelmed by tiredness. It was as if months and months of intense physical effort, of playing up to three games a week at the highest level, had finally caught up with me. Suddenly, even if I was just working on the physio's couch, I was knackered: I couldn't run any more, I couldn't sprint and I couldn't jump. I was shattered.

During the season I'd become accustomed to recharging my batteries in what little time I had with a siesta in the afternoon and then a good night's sleep. It was hardly ideal, but you also have to cram in family life and meetings with the press etc. In Laval, my body recovered steadily, and that fatigue that I'd been carrying through the season gradually drained away.

Still, my rehabilitation was going to take ages. You can't comprehend six months without being able to move properly. As much as anything else, it's unbelievably boring – what can you do when you can hardly walk? – but I knew I had to remain patient or I'd go out of my mind. The most difficult thing for me was to see my team-mates playing football. That was agonising; I simply couldn't bear it in the early weeks. I should have been out there with them, helping Arsenal win the championship and keeping the momentum going in the FA Cup. However, as I gradually fell into the rhythm of accepting my slow recovery, I felt able to watch the odd game on telly without driving myself insane with jealousy. In all honesty, I had to do something. I've never had so much time on my hands, just sitting around, watching telly or flicking through Stephen King novels.

The important thing is not to put on too much weight. I said earlier that an athlete's body is like a Formula One racing car, and that isn't a bad analogy. I realised when I was in my early twenties that to reach optimum performance every tiny part and detail must work perfectly in tandem. When you're injured you have to keep eating as you would normally when you're fit and well. You might not eat as much because you aren't burning as much of it off, sitting still all day, but all the nutritional levels you are used to have to stay the same. You have to take care of your body and give it the right fuel, just as you would if you were fit. Recuperation is impossible without the right diet.

I eat a huge amount of fish, sole in particular. Since the BSE crisis I've been extra careful about what I eat. At home my wife systematically reminds me what foods shouldn't be mixed together, like meat and starchy foods. Nathalie was with me every day during my recuperation and paid great attention to what I ate. I am very lucky that I live with someone who is so sympathetic to the rigorous demands of professional sport. While I am still paid to play football, our lives necessarily revolve around issues such as what we eat and where we live. That's not to say that I don't occasionally crack. During the closed season I sometimes give in to temptation and treat myself to a slice of cake – I'm only human, after all! But I never drink alcohol. Not even wine, which is hard for a Frenchman. I prefer to stick to water, the natural stuff.

Nathalie was also a huge help on the confidence front. I leant heavily on her during this time and will always be thankful for the support she gave me. The warmth and encouragement I received from those around me immediately after suffering the injury helped me during the frustrating months ahead. Whether it was from people I knew or complete strangers, they all improved my mood.

Of those I didn't know personally, there were thousands of French fans who left messages on the French Football Federation's website. There were letters of sympathy and encouragement as well, some of which were published in *L'Equipe* magazine. There was also my return to Highbury on 30 March 2002, just a week after my injury. That day, ironically enough, I received the Premiership's Player of the Month trophy and, with Nathalie there, the whole stadium gave me a standing ovation. It was incredibly touching. And I felt even better after my team-mates thrashed Sunderland 3–0. As I've said, for a player to watch a title race unfurl from the stands is incredibly difficult, but I was already dreaming of the final afternoon of the season on 11 May when I could stand as a member of this outstanding football team and lift the Premiership trophy.

Amazingly, and to my immense pride, among those who offered me best wishes in my recovery were the French president and prime minister, despite the fact that they were in the middle of a general election campaign. Jacques Chirac sent me a written message at Clairefontaine, Lionel Jospin phoned me. They both wished me a speedy recovery and urged me to remain positive; both also made a point of expressing their admiration for the way I had reacted to my setback. Their good wishes cheered me up. And at least my injury meant I could now follow the general election more closely while I spent my days recovering. I've always been very interested in politics, and the political situation at that time in France was fascinating. I meant it when I said that I would consider retiring from the national team if the far right-wing Jean-Marie Le Pen ever found himself in office. That would be unthinkable.

That kept my mind busy, reminding me that I couldn't just cry over what had happened to me. I didn't have the right. Sure, when Dr Jaeger had told me outright that I'd be out for six months, it had come as a real shock. But once that had sunk in, I thought to myself, 'Robert, you can't feel sorry for yourself. You still have the use of both your arms and both your legs. At the very worst you'll be playing football again in six months' time.' That's why I'll always go out of my way to support charities working on behalf of long-term patients, in particular those with rare illnesses like cystic fibrosis.

Missing out on the end of Arsenal's Double-winning season and being denied the chance to go to Asia as part of *Les Bleus'* squad hoping to defend our World Cup was a great shame. I had been desperate to take part and make an impact on the biggest tournament in the world, to participate in the most important event a professional footballer could ever know. But sometimes you just have to accept that what will be, will be. There you go. You've just got to get on with it.

While one half of North London spent the summer of 2002 recovering from the Double celebrations, I was in Saint-Raphaël working hard on my own recovery with Tiburce Darrou, a specialist trainer to whom Arsène Wenger often turns and who comes to work with us at Arsenal. After my spell at Laval, I'd finally gone under the knife in late April, and barely a week later, on 2 May, I set off for the south of France, following a path well trodden by Arsenal footballers in recent years. Arsène had taken to sending his crocked players down to Tiburce to undergo *à la carte* rehab; Rémi Garde had been the first, but other Gunners, French (Petit) and otherwise (Wright), had followed. Indeed, at the beginning of September I was joined by Freddie Ljungberg who was recovering from an operation on his hip. It was good to have some familiar company to work alongside.

I stayed at the Marina hotel in the port of Santa Lucia. My room overlooked the swimming pool with the sea beyond, but I hadn't come to the Côte d'Azur for a holiday. It might have been an idyllic setting, but I knew I was going to sweat buckets. This was going to be four months of hard labour.

Tiburce was going to help me 'reconstruct' my body. He's a giant, a huge man with a crop of shocking blond hair, but as a physical trainer he knows and understands an athlete's body and has worked over the years with big-name tennis players like Yannick Noah and Bjorn Borg. Tiburce has studied the mechanics of the body and supplements everything he's learned with his own innovative techniques. He stresses that you can't separate body and mind – a tired sportsman risks succumbing to injury. I'm living proof of that. He's also quick to put a positive spin on things. Keeping up morale and being optimistic is vital when you're stuck on the treatment table recuperating from a serious injury. I think I managed to keep my spirits up quite well throughout my time out of the game, always conscious that if the soul's in decent form, the body tends to follow.

But it was tough going with Tiburce. Every morning, at eight o'clock, I'd be on my bike facing a 40km cycle ride. Tiburce would choose a different course every day, each becoming steadily harder. I hadn't cycled much before; that summer I became something of an expert. Once the cycle ride was over, I'd turn up at the CERS (*Centre Européen de Rééducation du Sportif*) building, an ultra-modern gymnasium, for a work-out session on the knee itself aimed at steadily building up the strength in the joint. There'd be 20 minutes of exhausting work, after which I'd get a bit of a breather before lunch. Back at my club, training would normally finish by lunchtime, but not when you're recuperating *chez* Tiburce. After the meal, he'd take me out on to the running track in the stadium where there'd be more exercises, most of the runs incorporating jumping to test the knee's ability to cope with landing.

Tiburce came up with some horrible exercises to strengthen my knee. There'd be the 'stair' exercise, running up and down, over and over again. Then, to build up the strength in the whole leg, Tiburce would stand in front of me holding a football in both his hands, raising it steadily while I tried to touch it with my right knee, lifting my leg higher and higher to reach the ball.

It was only after around two months of this intensive work that I was able to work with a football again, dribbling and juggling. It was like being reunited with an old friend.

After that, my programme was a mixture of basic fitness work and technical exercises, all geared towards reinforcing my knee and bringing the fitness and strength levels in that leg back up to the levels of my body as a whole.

All those routines, coupled with the general fitness work on the bikes and the running track, slowly brought me back into shape. Every night I'd retire to my room absolutely knackered. I'd be shattered, and would even have difficulty walking for all the aches and pains inflicted by my sessions with Tiburce. But the results were there for all to see when I left his clinic: I was as good as new and nearing full fitness again after the long-term injury. I even went and visited my Arsenal team-mates on 13 August at London Colney, joining in with a few dribbles and ball-work games. That was something else, coming back to be with them.

Spending time at the rehab centre under Tiburce's watchful eye really helped me get through this. It allowed me to put things into perspective. I saw people there who were still suffering, who were facing years of recuperation and fitness work to return to the levels they'd been at in the past. Every time I got down to some work, I only had to look around me to remind myself that things could be worse.

As for my own recovery, I couldn't have been happier with the way things went. The treatment I received was second to none. Towards the middle of July there was even the possibility that I might return to competitive action in September rather than the long-anticipated October. In the end, though, common sense prevailed. Deep down I always knew I wouldn't be totally ready until October at the earliest, and ended up targeting our Champions League game with Auxerre on the 22nd of that month. I had to take my time, prepare myself properly and make sure the knee had completely healed after the operation. Being ready for competitive football is not just about being able to run again; you have to jump, tackle, shield the ball, dribble and be strong enough to shrug off challenges. I didn't want to take silly risks that might eventually set me back, and all just to be able to play in one or two games early in the season. My heart might have been urging me to get back playing as quickly as possible, but my head ruled the day. My body had to be ready. Thankfully, when Auxerre arrived in London that night, I had the feeling that it was.

I'll always remember the oration the fans gave me when I came off the bench that evening. I had other things on my mind at the time – we were trailing 2–0 and I was intent on preventing us slipping to a second successive defeat following our loss at Everton three days earlier.

That wasn't to be, but it was still a boost to be playing again. We went down 2–1 and I spent most of my time tearing around like a man possessed. Physically, I felt fine. I was tired, sure, and it was clear that it would take a while for me re-scale the technical heights I'd climbed to a year earlier, but it was promising.

At the final whistle I swapped shirts with Olivier Kapo, the striker who had scored Auxerre's first goal and with whom I'd become friendly while he was undertaking re-hab in Saint Raphael as well. It was ironic having him there at Highbury that night, effectively stealing my thunder.

I can't say right now whether I'll come back stronger or not. I'll only be able to answer that in May, but the signs are promising. After all the hard work and the fidgeting on the sidelines, it's just good to be back.

2

A First Step on the Ladder

Even now I remember it well. We were in a French lesson and we'd been given two hours to write an essay: 'What do you want to do when you're older?' I wrote that I wanted to be a professional footballer. I don't remember the reasons I gave, I basically just scribbled down my dreams; I might even have said that I wanted to win the World Cup, spurred on by the sight of Pelé and Maradona holding the trophy on the telly. I'm not saying this simply because I have been lucky enough to go on and achieve those ambitions, but because every young football fan dreams of doing just that. So I handed in my essay and thought nothing more of it.

Two weeks later the teacher gave me back the paper she'd marked. 'Robert, do you really consider being a professional footballer a proper job?' she asked.

'Yes, I think so,' I said.

'Well, it's not.'

It's funny looking back. She just dismissed it. I remember thinking to myself, 'We'll see.'

★

When you're young there's always someone to look up to, someone you want to be like when you're older. For me, it was my father Antonio.

He'd played a bit of football himself in his time, first in Portugal where he was born, then in France where he'd emigrated as a youngster. Even as a little kid I'd go with him, pestering him all the time to take me to his games. He'd play every Saturday afternoon and I would watch, happy to be with my dad. I'd put on my tiny football kit, take out my junior football and play with the other children who would be hanging around. From the age of five, 'going to football' was synonymous with running around having fun with my friends. Of course at that stage I wasn't thinking about becoming a professional player. I was just enjoying myself.

My father was less a role model and more of an idol for me. I wanted to do what he did. He was a forward, so that's where I played. I wanted to be able to run as fast as he did, I wanted to score as many goals as he did and to know how to dribble like he did. I would watch him playing for his factory team and I'd learn things – how to move around the pitch, even how much pleasure scoring a goal brought. Nowadays, I still benefit from those days as a kid watching from the sidelines. Everyone has to have an idol, and he was my first.

If my dad hadn't played himself, I don't think I would have developed my own passion for the game. If he'd gone another way, playing a different sport, I dare say I would have done the same. I certainly wouldn't have struggled as much as I have in order to reach the top in the game if he hadn't taken me with him every Saturday. What would I have done instead? Who knows? It's a question I often ask myself, but Dad decided to play football as an amateur. Thanks mainly to him, I now play professionally.

My father watches all my matches. He comes with my mother to London when they can. Of course, they don't see me play live as often as they did when I was playing at Metz, which was closer to home even than Reims, but I know that every time Arsenal games are on the telly, my father will find the channel and watch me play. It's still important for me that Dad offers me advice, telling me how he thought I played, and I respect his opinion: he's a football connoisseur.

But while I was definitely influenced by my father, I was lucky enough to be born with a gift. That's what my ability is, otherwise everyone would choose this profession. Others have a gift for writing, acting in the theatre, painting or baking cakes, but the talent still needs nurturing and a deal of hard work before it's any good to anyone.

My own dream took shape the day I joined my first club, Reims Sainte-Anne. From that moment on I began telling myself that I really would be a professional footballer one day. I was eight years old. Most people have dreams like this around this age – they may be to go to the moon or to drive a train. Mine was to play football, perhaps the hardest sport in which to reach the top level. Only a few people are actually successful because there is so much competition. But even at that young age, I played the game with a real intensity. Whenever I had a chance to score, I was oblivious to what was going on around me, though as soon as the match was over I'd click back into reality and the first people I'd usually see were my parents.

I was football crazy. Every year when they asked me what I wanted for my birthday or for Christmas, I'd always come back with the same reply: 'A football.' Someone, I don't remember who, bought me a foam ball and I'd kick it around the apartment, earn myself a smacked bottom and end up in tears. Looking back, it makes me laugh; that ball left a trail of devastation around the flat until one day, suddenly and mysteriously, it disappeared. My suspicions still rest with my mother – she was always cursing about it – but to this day she's not confessed.

You need someone else around, a partner in crime so to speak, like a brother or sister to play with. Enter my younger brother Tony. The pair of us received the perfect upbringing, harsh but fair. We'd give the same stories to our parents that all children try and, of course, they'd see through them all and yell at us. We'd play with the foam ball inside and then, when Mum got home demanding to know who broke this and who broke that, my brother and I just blamed each other and took responsibility for nothing. She'd eventually flip her lid and would smack us both.

We were a really solid, functioning family unit and I owe a lot of my success to that. My brother works with my father now in the Valeo motorcar parts factory near Reims. We don't play football together any more – not because of who I am or what I've achieved, but because I hardly ever have time to be with them, so when we do see each other we've got so much to catch up on we don't really have the time to kick a ball around. Anyway, when I'm really on holiday the last thing I want to do is play football.

Nowadays I often stop and watch youngsters playing in the street or in parks, if only because every professional can recall doing the same. I remember the sense of freedom having a kick-about with your mates can give you; it didn't matter what position you played. People used to stop and watch us play too. Now it's role reversal. Any sport gives you that sense of freedom. When you're playing competitively, you concentrate on the game and think of nothing else. Over the course of a game of football you forget everything apart from what's going on immediately around you in the game for 90 minutes, and I don't think it was all that different when I was a kid. I still enjoy myself, but when I'm playing all that's important to me is beating the opposing team.

Despite having lived in France all my life, I still feel a huge affinity with my father's country of birth, and I went back to Portugal after Euro 2000. It was a chance to come back down to earth after we beat Italy in the final. Up there in the mountains around Oporto, it's a totally different world to the hustle and bustle of Paris or London.

My family own a house just outside Ponte de Lima where I go to get away from it all, find tranquillity and just clear my head. When my brother and I were small, we'd come here with our parents for summer holidays. It was a 2,000km journey travelling in a stuffy little car and at the time there were no motorways to speed things up. There was one border crossing for God knows how many cars and we'd sit there for hours in the jam. But that didn't matter. Crammed in the car in that heat, we were just really happy and excited to be on holiday. Ponte de Lima, a little village near Oporto, came to be a very special place for my family. We'd all be together there, with my cousins dropping round every night. Even now, that little house doesn't have a television or a telephone, and it's still not a bad place to chill out. It's nice to see no one else other than my family for four or five days once in a while. I can find more peace and quiet up there than anywhere else in the world.

José Fernandez is my uncle and godfather and plays an important part in my family's footballing history. He played for Stade de Reims and once earned himself rave reviews from Raymond Kopa, the Michel Platini of the 1950s who helped France to third place at the 1958 World Cup finals in Sweden. José should have been playing regularly in the first team, so in him I see everything good and bad about the game: good because he was so naturally talented and was great to watch, but bad because he wasted that talent.

I get on well with José and I don't want to judge him. If he decided to party instead of working on his game, that's because no one advised him otherwise, and he probably had a great time too. I almost went the same way between the ages of 18 and 20; at that age you and your mates start to crave freedom, you discover girls, you go clubbing and get in at four or five in the morning even when you have to play the next afternoon. That was the path José took, and there was no one there to hold him back. Thanks to my mother, I didn't get far down that road. She was hard on me, but I thank her for that now. She'd keep asking me, 'What do you want? I get the impression you don't actually want to be a professional footballer. Do you want to end up like your uncle?'

In that sense, José was a good example to me, a good example of how I didn't want to end up and a constant reminder of the sacrifices that were necessary. He'd had lots of fun when he was younger, but he hadn't been able to live out his passion: to turn professional. He had touched his dream, but it ended up passing him by. He still plays now, but it's only for the steelworks factory team where he works. He could have done so much more with his ability. I wanted to turn my dream into reality, and if that meant sacrificing a few nights out with the lads, then fair enough. When I did go out, I made sure I was back home by one o'clock while my friends stayed out all night. That hurts when you're only 17 or 18, but I'm thankful now.

With a Portuguese father, a Benfica fan born near Oporto, and a Spanish mother from Oviedo who supported Real Madrid, my background was about as Latin as it comes. My mother Mabel was the strict one. My father let a bit more go, but Mum was always there fretting about our future. I would say to her, 'Mum, just leave me alone. I'm fed up with you looking over my shoulder all the time. I just want to be who I am.' But she's a determined woman – like mother, like son – and has that stubborn, passionate streak that typifies people from the South. I've got her to thank for the path my career took compared to that of my uncle José.

I remember coming home one evening from training at Stade de Reims and announcing that I'd had enough of football. Suffice to say, that didn't go down too well. My mother was so livid she couldn't even bring herself to hit me. Initially she didn't say anything while she came to terms with the bombshell I'd just dropped, then she launched into one. 'You're no better than a good for nothing,' she screamed. 'You don't know what you want, and you're not going to succeed in life if you think you don't have to work for things. No, from now on you're on your own. I can't be bothered with you! We're not going to do you any favours from now on in.'

Now, I share my mother's fiery Mediterranean temperament and some of the rows we had were quite spectacular. As a child, people thought I was too frail to play football but I'd go out with older friends of mine and play anyway. I was from the stubborn South, and when I decided to do something, that's exactly what I did. And I'm close to my mother because of that. I always telephone her before a game. It's become a ritual; if I didn't do it, she'd panic and fret over me. I'm always fine and everything's always going well, but I'm obliged to call her to put her mind at rest. It's usually an hour and a half before kick-off, more often than not while we're on the coach between the team hotel and the stadium. I'll give her a quick call on my mobile. I've never forgotten. Even when I was with France in Japan for the

Confederations Cup in June 2001, I'd call her. The conversation is always exactly the same.

'Mum, it's me.'

'Are you all right?'

'Yes.'

'Good. Have a good game.'

It takes ten seconds. That's all.

You tend to see footballers with their ears constantly glued to mobiles. We need them because we are usually on the road, travelling to one game or another, and they have become invaluable in all walks of life. For our generation, the mobile has become something that we can't live without, a means of checking in a couple of minutes that your loved ones are fine.

Apart from my family, my other major influence when I was a kid was the Spanish international Michel. I remember the first time I saw him play for that massive club Real Madrid. He oozed so much talent and was so graceful. I was mesmerised. I loved the way he moved when he was in possession, inspiring those around him from midfield, where I also played. He was such a good all-round player. His balance, his vision and his class all struck me the first time I saw him and I always followed him after that. At Reims, in the junior and youth teams, we decided not to call ourselves by our own names but by the names of our favourite players. The other members of my side called me Michel. It was just a bit of fun, but I used to get so much pleasure from pretending I was him. I think it's something all kids do.

I have never met him. If I had the chance, I'd tell him how I've admired his play since I was a lad to the extent that I had photos and posters of him plastered around my bedroom. It's good to identify with someone. Of course, as my game developed, my style of play was not a carbon copy of Michel's, but as a youngster he had been a source of inspiration. It's interesting that I chose a Spanish footballer rather than a Frenchman. I must have been influenced by my holidays in Spain with my mother's family, and above all by watching Real Madrid play on the television and seeing Michel run with that elegant swagger wearing that distinctive white shirt. Back then I'd never have dreamt that one day that very same club would try to sign me.

For a young player with ambition, the best clubs are not always the biggest clubs. When you're setting out as a footballer between eight and 14, the age when you start dreaming you can forge yourself a professional career, the best club is more often than not your local side. That's the path I followed.

Sainte-Anne was the first rung on the ladder. I signed there at eight years old, and six years later would go on to join Stade de Reims, the main team in the region. Reims have run into tough times recently, languishing in the French lower leagues; they had their heyday in the 1950s when Kopa inspired them to reach the 1956 European Cup final, which they lost 4–3 to, guess who, Real Madrid. If I'd gone straight to Stade de Reims at eight years old I doubt I would have had such a good time. A club like Sainte-Anne allows you to enjoy your football; at Reims I'd have been in a fiercely competitive environment straight away. First and foremost, at that age it is about having fun. At Sainte-Anne, if we won it was great, but if we lost it was great too. There was no pressure to get a result, and, in my opinion, it is far easier for a youngster to start off at an amateur club of little reputation than in a big-name team.

You should never forget your roots, and I'm still in contact with a few of my team-mates from Sainte-Anne. Unfortunately, no one else made it into the big time – of my generation, I was the only one – but we still had a good side and were even French junior champions, beating Bastia in the final at Parc des Princes. Our game was the warm-up act for the French Cup final in 1983 between PSG and Nantes (the Parisians won 3–2). That wasn't a bad first appearance on the larger stage.

I didn't score that day, though I did hit the post. Back then I played up front and I notched up on average around 20 goals a season, forming the ideal strike force with my partner. He was big and strong, I was small and quick. Occasionally nowadays when I score, I have flashbacks to similar goals I scored as a youth player. Nothing much seems to have changed in between.

My first coach was called Bernard Rouselle and he was a great early influence on my career. He won quite a few titles with my age group and he took me under his wing. If I ever get the chance I'd like to introduce Bernard to Arsène Wenger. Arsène played in amateur football at Mutzig in Alsace before joining Mulhouse and Strasbourg as a professional. He then trained the youngsters at RC Strasbourg before leaving for Cannes, then Monaco, then Japan. Bernard would admire such steady progress, and I'd love to be a fly on the wall if ever they met up.

The fact that there aren't as many dedicated volunteer youth-team coaches like Bernard in France these days worries me. They are the most important people for young players, not only in football but in any sport. We should be helping them and encouraging them to get out there to coach the kids, because that is where the professional players of the future are going to be found.

We always make a point of praising the professional game for its contribution to the development of the sport, but the amateur set-up is the grass-roots of football. My roots are in amateur football and it provided me with the basis on which to build my career. When I was at Sainte-Anne, my coach didn't earn a penny; he donated his time to us for free. We should be thanking them, though it shouldn't be down to us, the professional players, to give money directly to the smaller clubs. That should be the responsibility of the state. For us, football is a job and we already pay half our salary back to the government in taxes. That's fair enough, but the government departments involved should redirect some of those monies back into the grass-roots of the game and subsidise amateur clubs.

They actually named the stadium at Sainte-Anne after me, an honour usually bestowed only on someone who's dead. But they decided to make an exception after I earned my first France cap, and the ground where I made my debut now bears my name. They asked me what I thought before they announced it, but what can you say? That's where I learned the team game that I love; it made me very proud. There's also a Robert Pires Way in the village of Petit Ebersviller, near Macheren in the Moselle. The road leads to the local stadium, a gentle reminder that that's where they'd like me to end up one day, back home near Metz. It's a nice thought, and the not so subtle hint makes me chuckle.

I'm proud that I come from Reims, where I was born on 29 October 1973. Even now, wherever I am in the world, I look out for Stade de Reims' results from afar, hoping they might earn promotion from the National League into the Second Division. Reims and the area around the town are beautiful and relatively affluent. It baffles me sometimes why some of the bigger champagne houses from the region don't invest some of their money in the local team. Reims could do with a little financial nudge in the right direction. Sure, everyone knows about champagne, but football brings a town to people's attention in a different way. It's frustrating to see the team struggle financially when it's surrounded by such wealth.

Much as a wine specialist tours the local vineyards looking for the best wines, the bigger regional clubs scout around at the smaller teams to find the cream of the talent. I was spotted playing for Sainte-Anne by a Stade de Reims scout, and at the end of the season they approached me and offered me the chance to join them for the following season. Having discussed the move with my parents, I agreed.

So, at the age of 14, I was snapped up by Stade de Reims. It was a wrench to leave Sainte-Anne and Bernard Rouselle in particular, but he was proud of what I had achieved and told me, 'If you've been picked out by Stade de Reims it's because you have the talent. You deserve this success.' Stade de Reims only took the best local young players, and while I hadn't achieved anything yet, it was a fillip to be asked to join them. I was clearly going in the right direction. Coincidentally, Stade's colours – red shirts with white sleeves – are the same as Arsenal's. I wonder whether I'll wear the Reims colours again towards the end of my career? We'll have to see.

Not that I made a particularly convincing start at the club. I'd become used to the homely atmosphere of Sainte-Anne and this was a different world, and when you've been scouted and picked out at the age of 14 it can easily go to your head. You think you're a star, that you've made it; in that respect, that first season proved something of a rude awakening for me and left me mentally and physically drained. On the pitch I'd moved back into the hole in attacking midfield, but the step up in competition was too much and completely threw me. That was why I considered quitting: I was used to being the team's star player and it was tough to be asked to prove myself all over again.

At the time, the youth set-up was divided into three teams – A, B and C. I stayed in the C group, the worst, for three weeks. At that age, when you're still harbouring real aspirations of turning professional one day, to find yourself in with the no-hopers really hurts. But just when I was thinking I'd had enough, I was picked to captain the team in the Gambardella Cup, albeit only in the early stages of the competition. It was the first time, at any level, that I'd been made captain and I can remember even now the thrill it gave me. It seemed things were looking up until midway through the second half, when I got myself sent off for a bad tackle and ended up being yelled at in the dressing room for letting the side down. Predictably enough, my mother had a real go at me when I got home, and quite rightly so. Not a great start in your first game as skipper.

As a young footballer trying to make it in a professional league, you find yourself in a dog eat dog world. The clubs make no bones about the fact that if you don't make it, it's no skin off their nose. They can just go and find someone else who might. They're brutal, and you quickly have to learn how to survive and have the strength of will to want to succeed, come what may. My family helped me in that respect, convincing me that if I'd been spotted and signed up in the first place, it must be because I had the talent they were looking for. They believed in me, so why shouldn't I believe in myself?

Academically, I was nothing more than average, so my parents were advised to send me to the Colbert High School in Reims to take sports studies. At the start of the academic year, I sat the entrance exams to get into the *lycée sport-études* (it wasn't just a matter of walking into the place), fortunately passed them and began a two-year course. The people at Colbert really helped me, pushing me in the right direction. I don't believe in fate, but I was certainly lucky to end up there, under the guidance of people who understood me and really wanted to get the best out of me. Some people are fortunate enough to be talented at school as well as at sport, but I wasn't one of them. I struggled with the academic side of things, but Colbert, with a decent football team and a sports studies course that kept me engaged, was the ideal environment for me.

Two years later, as I approached my 17th birthday, I'd hit my academic limit but I was excelling at sport. That much was clear, so I opted out of school to concentrate on my football. I'd never been particularly bothered about my lessons. I'd taken Spanish as my first language and English as my second, but you'd never guess it listening to me now, even though I live in England. A decent education is important and becomes even more so if you don't make it in the game, but at some stage you have to make a choice: sport or studies. It's hard to do both and it's up to each individual to work out what he or she can manage. Life's all about choices, and sometimes you make the wrong one. I'd say only about three or four per cent of the people who made the choice I did ended up making it in the game.

Dominique Perquin, my first trainer at Stade de Reims, was an astute tactical judge and passionate about the game. He stuck by me through that difficult first year, and did the same the following season when I'd been promoted to the first team but found myself more often than not sitting on the bench. He didn't make me a special case. His priority, and the club's emphasis as well, was with the academy players. I was just an amateur, contracted to Stade and enlisted on a sports studies course in town. The next step for me was to get myself into the academy, though only once I'd finished my course.

It was Perquin who took the decision to take me on and sign me up to the academy, which came as a relief because I was finding it difficult to juggle my studies and my football. He offered me an apprentice contract at Stade, which I signed, and at 17 I started picking up my first wages as a footballer. I was told to collect my pay cheque from the cashier's desk and, having been handed a slip for 796FF (around £80), I sprinted home proudly clinging to the scrap of paper before shoving it in my mother's face. 'Look, Mum! I've got my first pay cheque! I'm on my way now!'

I remember playing a Third Division game for Stade de Reims against Baumes-Isle on 11 January 1992. We were losing 1–0, but I equalised and scored the winner with seven minutes to go. (I can even remember the team that day: Bompard, Dufour, Diaz (Cardoso, 40), Melloni, Guion, Larchet, Monier, Diop (Ekollo, 75), Pires, Gace, Bollini, with my goals coming after 48 and 83 minutes.) At the end everyone came up to congratulate me, saying I'd played a blinder. That evening we met up with the coach Pierre Phelipon to celebrate in the usual way. And that's when it hit me. I was 18 years old, I'd just scored two goals and I felt like a star. For the first time in my life, I felt the pure adrenalin of success. That night I was the hero, everyone was happy for me and wanted to be with me. I was surrounded by friends and team-mates and we drank, we went clubbing, we met girls . . .

This was a crucial moment for me, and I believe it comes at some point to every successful footballer. It's a matter of balancing your ego with your talent and ensuring the ego never grows more quickly than the talent. You've got to keep your feet on the ground or you'll fail. I watch young footballers now, bursting with natural talent, and will them to have the common sense to listen to the senior pros and coaching staff around them. The dangers are greater now than they were in my day. The media, agents, sponsors and the like will throw money and fame at young players before they know how to handle it.

Being a footballer was my vocation in life. Now I've achieved that, but my motivation is to remain a professional through and through. I followed the right path. If I'm honest, I'd love to bump into that French teacher who dismissed my ambition so easily all those years ago. I might even treat myself to a wry smile.

3

In the Maroon of Metz

As a youth-team player, you approach the end of your second season with a real sense of dread. That's when the club announces the retained list, those youngsters who are to progress into the professional ranks. You are called into the manager's office and told either you've made it or you are to be released. No one ever bothers mentioning your actual professional contract. It's just 'You're staying' or 'Thanks, but no thanks'.

The whole experience is traumatic. I remember the expression on the faces of those who had been released, some of whom you'd never see again. Nowadays people come up to me and say, 'You footballers, you've got it made. You've got everything you want, you earn lots of money . . .' People have no idea of the stress involved, or what the players have gone through during years of training, or the sacrifices they've made to get where they are. It's a massive disappointment to be told, after all that, that you've not made it. Football's not all about fast cars and glamorous lifestyles. There's a flip side to all that. I've seen

18-year-olds burst into tears when they're told they're not to be offered a contact. It's not as glitzy as it seems.

★

My experiences immediately after joining Reims, when I'd found myself down the pecking order and on the fringes of the side, had shown me that this would be no easy ride. True to form, having entered the academy I found myself back on the bench. For a footballer, watching from the sidelines makes you feel effectively jobless, in a kind of limbo. You feel useless, helpless, unable to show what you can do out on the pitch. You have to wait until the coach gives you a chance, so it's all about patience and being ready for whenever that moment comes.

At that stage of my career, I'd only ever been a regular at Sainte-Anne; at Reims I had to fight for a place. Sure, I had earned myself a place at the youth academy, but I was playing in the old Third Division. During the 1991/92 season I played five matches at that level, scoring two goals, but still found myself dropped back to a lower level of the local regional league for several matches. I spent my season being shunted from one league to the other.

That year, Reims had run into financial problems, and after months of rumours the club finally filed for bankruptcy in the autumn of 1991. From mid-season, we had to play in the knowledge that regardless of where we finished in the table we'd be relegated because of the financial mess at the club. We ended up sixth in the Eastern section of the Third Division but, as feared, dropped into the local regional league. Almost all the professional players had abandoned ship by then, which meant we were left with a pretty inexperienced squad and a struggling team.

Before the end of the season, Reims filed for bankruptcy for a second time and things looked really desperate. This time all the players, including me, had had enough of the uncertainty, and once that season was over we went for trials all over the place. It was a pretty scary time for all of us. Everything was up in the air and none of us knew where we'd be playing, if anywhere, the following season. I began ringing round clubs frantically to see if they were interested in me. Valenciennes took me on trial for a couple of days, but then never called me back. So I carried on training with Reims until I met Robert Sarre, a scout covering the area between Reims and Metz.

Robert is the main talent-spotter in the area around Reims and he puts most promising players Metz's way. He'd had his eye on me for a while and eventually came to see my parents and asked whether I'd be interested in joining Metz. Of course I was! Joining a club of their size and stature – they're probably the French equivalent of Aston Villa or Everton – was the next natural step forward for me, and after all the uncertainty at Reims it came as a timely boost.

A fortnight later Robert Sarre, my mother and father and I met Francis de Taddeo, the head of Metz's youth academy. Even today Francis plays an important role at the club: as well as a coach, he acts as caretaker manager for the first team when necessary and was in charge of the club for

a few days in the winter of 2002. We met at the Tincqueux
Novotel hotel. I remember it as if it were yesterday; it was
a meeting that shaped my future. Francis produced a
contract from his briefcase and offered me a two-year deal
with an option for a further year if Metz was pleased with
my progress. If not, I'd be out on my ear. I don't know
why, but my reaction was to turn to the academy director
and ask, 'Don't you even want me to do a trial?' I'd just had
a trial at Valenciennes and failed to impress, so I naively
thought that Metz would be sure to want to have a proper
look at me. Francis de Taddeo just smiled and said he had a
confidence in Robert Sarre's judgement. I signed and, a few
months later, I started at the Metz youth academy. It was
the beginning of six happy years wearing the maroon of FC
Metz.

Reims had been hard at first, but this was a step up again.
I spent the summer holidays at Ponte de Lima with my
family, but my thoughts were dominated by the adventure
that awaited me at my new club. I was now a proper
apprentice footballer. At Reims it had felt as though I was
part of an amateur football club, but at Metz the set-up was
far more professional with greater care and attention paid to
the well-being and development of the young players. That
was the main difference. The financial problems at Reims
ensured there was no continuity between youth team and
the senior staff, and it was clear the youth academy had lost
its way. In the end it was closed down. The buildings are
still there, but they're now used as student accommodation
for the university.

The visiting Newcastle fans give me an unsympathetic send-off as I depart Highbury in agony on a stretcher following my injury.

The happiest day of my club career. Lifting the FA Barclaycard Premiership trophy following our league success. Even with my knee in a brace, to have finally won a title after coming so close at Metz and Marseille was the fulfilment of a dream.

My childhood was spent in Champagne, though even then my passion for European football shone through. I swapped the Barcelona kit (centre left) for the colours of Porto (bottom right) when on holiday at Ponte de Lima in Portugal. My father, a Benfica fan, was unimpressed.

(*Above*) On the road to greatness. My first appearance at Parc des Princes, playing for Reims Sainte-Anne in the French Junior Cup final. Though I hit the woodwork, we won the game before settling to watch PSG beat Nantes 3-2 in the French Cup final proper afterwards.
(*Below*) With my team-mates after that first trophy success.

Playing and wearing the captain's armband for the first time in the red and white of Stade de Reims, and with my team-mates (kneeling third from right). It makes me smile to think I'd end up wearing those same colours again at Arsenal.

Enrolled at the Lycée Colbert at Stade de Reims, I chose to quit my studies in pursuit of becoming a professional footballer at the age of 17.

(*Above*) Captaining L'OM against Metz. We drew 1-1 that night during my difficult second season at the Stade Vélodrome as our campaign lurched from bad to worse.

(*Left*) Renewing acquaintances with my former Metz coach Joël Muller.

(*Below*) Every footballer's ultimate dream. Kissing the World Cup on 12 July, 1998 following our exhilarating 3-0 victory over Brazil. With images of Pelé, Maradona and other legends of the game whizzing around my head, I didn't want to hand the trophy to the next man. An unbelievable night.

(*Right*) With my mother Mabel, my father Antonio and my younger brother Tony in Portugal in 1988. We are a really solid, functioning family and I owe a lot of my success to them.

(*Below*) With Nathalie at the 52nd Cannes Film Festival in May 1999. She keeps my feet on the ground.

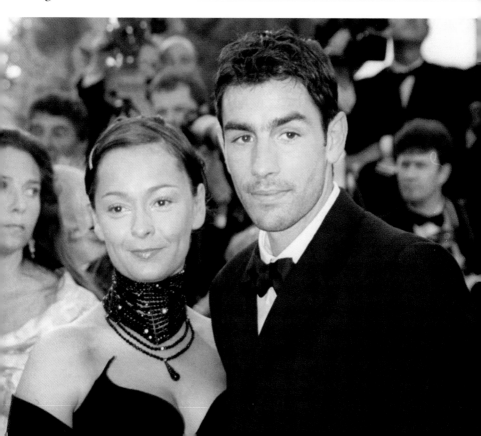

(*Above left*) Celebrating after scoring one of the best goals of my career to give us the lead at Aston Villa in March 2002.(*Above right*) With Sylvain Wiltord, a quality player who has come into his own with Arsenal, during the 2-1 win at Villa Park. (*Below*) Celebrating with Patrick Vieira after he had scored our third goal during the 4-1 win over Bayer Leverkusen in February 2002. In a competition as strong as the Champions League, results like that come along only once in a blue moon.

Life at Metz's academy was much stricter. You had to be on time everywhere, whether that meant on the pitch, for meals or for meetings with the coach. Everything was carefully scheduled, drumming home the need to be disciplined, with either lessons or training sessions all day. At Reims we'd trained every morning and on Tuesday and Wednesday afternoons. On Thursday and Friday afternoons we'd had various classes so that we did not fall behind too much on basic schooling, but the classes weren't compulsory and you could take them or leave them. I didn't bother going. While I appreciate now how important it is, back then I wasn't interested and preferred to go into town and enjoy myself. But it was a different world at Metz. All of us had the same hopes and aspirations, but we knew full well that we wouldn't all make it. The competition was tough. The day was very timetabled and would start pretty early. It was like being at boarding school, in as much as we were away from home and living in an institution with lots of rules. We hardly ever got to go out with our mates and our whole existence was focused on football. Effectively we had committed ourselves to a profession which was not making any promises. We were still not earning proper money and we lived in constant uncertainty, unsure from one day to the next whether or not we were going to get dumped. Except for weekends, when there were trips and matches, days passed as if we were living in military barracks; orders were barked at us and we had to obey them. Having been through military service as a teenager, it all felt pretty familiar to me. I knew the drill and, looking back, discipline taught me how to live in a group, something that is essential for every professional footballer.

Like that of any trade, a footballer's apprenticeship is divided into stages. You've got to be tough, refusing to give up, each stage preparing you for the next which is, inevitably, that little bit tougher – just like each division is a bit harder than the last when you've turned pro. The teachers and the coaches won't do you any favours, and you're aware that you're actually competing against your team-mates so there's not much personal support there. At the beginning it is hard – you can't do as you please like you could before, you're in an alien environment, you've lost your bearings and you miss your family. When you are told to be somewhere at a certain time you have to make sure you're there or else the bus just leaves without you and you look like an idiot. Little things like that teach you how to live and to be disciplined.

I was almost 19 years of age when I arrived at the academy in a city where I didn't know a soul. In the early days I missed my family and friends; they visited me occasionally, but they had their own lives to lead. My parents were still living near Reims and we only saw each other every fortnight, for four hours on a Sunday before they'd have to return home. Apart from their brief visits, I was on my own.

When you're a teenager, that's not easy. Maybe things have changed; players are given more support these days. Nevertheless, then as now, you are still out on your own, ever conscious that the lads with whom you share your meals are there, like you, to succeed. They will do anything to make the grade themselves, and would happily step on you if it meant taking your place in the team.

Given the atmosphere, then, it was a pretty big moment in my fledgling career when, as we stood in a little stadium on the outskirts of the city watching a Metz side competing in the regional league, Robert Sarre turned to me and said, 'Come with me, Robert. Let's go and meet the chairman. I'll introduce you to him.'

He was standing by himself behind the goal and we strolled round the pitch to where he was.

'Mr Molinari, I would like to introduce you to Robert Pires from Reims,' said Robert. 'Mark my words, he's going to be a great player.'

Carlo Molinari looked at me and replied, 'I look forward to him proving it.'

He had set me a challenge. In my first two years at Metz I felt I did myself justice working under my coach Philippe Hinschenberger, a former FC Metz player. I trusted him completely and became a regular for him in the reserves, playing well while still attending the academy. Other coaches I came across would comment on my speed and technique, but Philippe saw something different in the way I played. He wanted to use me less as a central midfielder and more as a winger, or even at times as an out-and-out forward.

I was clearly doing something right. While I was playing in the reserves Mr Molinari received an offer from Benfica for me. He was quite open about it, telling me he'd received the fax — some chairmen prefer to keep negotiations under wraps when they get offers for their players, but that was not

Carlo's way – and despite the size of the transfer fee proposed, he made it clear he was going to turn it down.

As it was, that didn't bother me that much because things were progressing well at Metz and Philippe Hinschenberger soon handed me over to Joël Muller, the first-team manager. At first Joël came down quite hard on me, partly because I was doing well on the pitch and the newspapers were talking about me, but also because he wanted to protect me. He wanted me to develop at my own pace and really fulfil my potential. He may not agree, but he was tough with me, and I suppose, with hindsight, that was the kind of treatment I needed. If life had been easier I might never have achieved what I have in the game.

Throughout my career I've always had someone behind me, supporting me. Joël took over where Philippe left off. If I got above my station – say, for instance, if I bought a flash car – he would be quick to put me in my place. One day he called me into his office and, casting a glance towards the parking lot, asked me, 'What's that car? You can't buy that. Who do you take yourself for?' Suffice to say I suddenly felt rather ashamed of my new top-of-the-range Mercedes. He would fine me for being late for training, for talking too much, for whatever he wanted. Once I did a newspaper interview on my likes and dislikes, and under the 'Don't like' column I had put training on Tuesday mornings as it was too rigorous. Joël read the article and before the session called me in.

'What's all this about?' he asked. 'You don't like Tuesday mornings?'

'No, not much,' I replied.

He fined me.

Even now the memory of those Tuesday mornings sends shivers down my spine. I'd turn up for training knowing that I was going to be absolutely exhausted by the end of the day. There were two horrendous fitness sessions – one in the morning, one in the afternoon – to prepare us for Saturday's match and ensure we'd be able to see out 90 minutes. I hated them.

The academy coaches are well aware that they are dealing with players who are still essentially boys and whose bodies are still changing. Their job is to ensure that the exercise, weight-training and stamina work they have you doing give you the strength to see you through 90 minutes of competitive football. When I arrived at Metz, the difference in the physical effort that was required of me was obvious from the outset. Mid-week training was aimed at building up stamina, the sessions on Tuesday and Wednesday particularly harsh. Between the ages of 18 and 20 you feel real pain. There'd be different ball-juggling routines which we learned as if they were scales on a piano, but once those basic skills were second nature we'd turn to weight-training to increase body strength. At the same time you are trying to perfect your balance, which isn't easy given that your body is developing and thickening out. Weight-training sessions became more intense and pre-season training was harder and longer each year. It can make you miserable, but the thought of playing and working on skills keeps you going. At Metz the physical aspects of our preparation were all important; as in any job, there is a time when you have to put in real effort to get to the top.

When I signed for Metz, I was initially asked to fill a role as playmaker in the team. I had done as much at Reims, playing behind the strikers, but Philippe Hinschenberger needed someone to play on the left side of midfield in the reserves. I drew the short straw, but I must have done all right because they left me there from then on in. When I was eventually promoted to the first team that's where I played. I wasn't allowed to drift out of position at all, which was fair enough because the manager had a rigid formation that worked for him.

I actually loved it, charging up and down the left touchline and running at the opponents' full-back, and as time went on they trusted me more and I was given more freedom to express myself. I stayed at Metz for six years, and by the 1997/98 season I was doing more or less what I wanted. It's another example of a scrap of good fortune falling my way. What if the coach had gone for someone else to fill that role? I might have continued to develop as a playmaker, but just as likely I might not have made it at all. When you get a break, you must make the best of it.

I've got a lot to thank Joël Muller for. I owe him so much. He was a great influence on me in my early years, mainly because he had faith in me. He was a very hard worker who loved his job and devoted considerable time to it, so I'm not at all surprised at what he has managed to achieve since, most notably coming so close to winning the championship at Lens and keeping them challenging at the top of the French league. He's the consummate professional with discipline at the forefront of his style, and he taught me to be the same way. Joël was also a creature of habit and tended to stick to routines. His team line-up was always read out in the same room at the Saint-Symphorien stadium; if his meeting clashed with a seminar in that room, he would have it cancelled or ask for it to be allocated elsewhere. Similarly, he'd always request the same hotel room when we went off for mini-breaks.

Life's never predictable, and maybe his routines were some kind of trick he used to help him feel he was in total control of the situation. Back then, at the very beginning of my career, I was a little superstitious too. We'd stay at the Novotel hotel before home games and I always asked for the same room, number 329. My room-mate was David Terrier who, as luck would have it, also subsequently came to play in England with Newcastle and West Ham.

But if I'm not superstitious any more, I do firmly believe in God. We are here because we have been given the gift of life. Everyone has a talent, whether it be for acting, writing, drawing or building, and those gifts come from somewhere and from someone. Then there are those momentous events in life, like the untimely death of a loved one. Fabien, one of my best friends, was killed in a car crash a few years ago, but I still think about him a great deal. It was a very painful loss; we were best friends as kids and I know his family well. But I know that I'll see him again one day, not in this world, but in another. I have faith in God and in myself, and I cross myself when I run out on to the pitch, even if I do it very discreetly.

I was initially on a two-year apprenticeship at Metz, though they ended up bypassing the third-year option and signing me up as a fully fledged professional on a four-year deal. That said a lot. The third year of an apprenticeship is normally used to prepare players for the professional game, but I didn't have that 'breaking-in' period and was instead plunged straight in at the deep end. Whilst I was still actually a second-year apprentice Joël Muller put his trust in me and, despite my lack of experience, thought I could be an integral part of the team. I was barely 20, but during that 1993/94 season I was a regular in the first team with the manager referring to me as his 'key player'. The newspapers picked up on that and my name began to crop up more and more. It was all a completely new experience for me and, looking back, maybe there was too much responsibility and too much pressure put on me to perform.

The start of the season was a disaster. We lost at home on the opening day and were beaten away in our next match before scraping a point at home and then another away. It was only early September but we already had a vital game against Le Havre that we simply had to win. Before that game, Carlo Molinari decided to sign Philippe Vercruysse, a former French international and an established star at Lens and Marseille, to add more punch to our forward line. It proved a masterstroke. Philippe shouldered all the responsibility, taking the pressure off me in the process, and the team suddenly clicked. I played alongside him and just off him, but his presence gave me a free rein and helped me grow up, prompting an amazing season.

He also helped team spirit. I'm someone who doesn't have too much trouble fitting well into a group, and I'm no troublemaker, though I've changed over the years. When I was younger I was very shy, staying on the fringes and listening to others tell their stories and jokes. I wasn't a loner – you can't distance yourself from the other lads, and if you feel better keeping yourself to yourself you should play tennis, not football – but I've never fought to be the centre of attention and am quite happy to let others do the talking. On joining Metz, it took me quite a while to strike up any really close friendships. All my mates were still in Reims. But, with time, I gradually struck up a friendship with Bruno Rodriguez, who went on to play in England with Bradford City. He had a Corsican temperament, completely different to mine, but we got on very well and saw each other a fair bit off the field. I also got on well with David Zitelli (now plying his trade in Scotland, at Hearts) and Cyril Pouget, and, after I had broken into the first team, players like Anthony Baffoe and Philippe Chanlot helped me out. They were model professionals and, as a young pretender in among them, to have their backing meant a lot.

There was a real team spirit, particularly in training. We had a system of fines for latecomers, and at the end of my last two seasons at the club I took my place on the latecomers' podium of shame in second place behind Rigobert Song. He had to pay 2,000FF (about £200) for his lack of punctuality, with me trailing in with 1,600FF (£160). Joël Muller stuck the results up on the noticeboard and liked to remind us how much we owed. 'Rigo', who went on to play for Liverpool and West Ham and is now back in France with Lens, had a flat on the same landing as me in Metz. He had number six and I had number seven, so we'd often be late together. 'Is this how you set an example to the youngsters?' Joël Muller would ask, exasperated. 'Who do you think you are? So much for discipline.'

I really found my footballing feet at Metz. It was a very good time for me. As I have already mentioned, while I was there the Portuguese club Benfica tried to sign me, but the club weren't interested in selling me. I would have turned them down anyway. I wasn't ready to leave. I'd only just got to Metz who had gone out of their way to sign me up when I'd been going nowhere at Reims. At that stage I didn't see myself ever leaving, especially not abroad which really scared me, even if it was to my father's team, Benfica. Joël Muller gave me his opinion at the time. 'You shouldn't leave,' he said. 'You're still learning. It isn't the right thing to do.' The chairman showed me the offer, but I always got the impression he was going to turn them down anyway.

It's hard for me to give advice to young French players who are approached to go abroad, but a youngster's footballing education is important and should not be cut short. If a young player of 18 wants to go to Spain or Italy, that's up to him, but afterwards he shouldn't come back crying and looking for another club, complaining that French clubs aren't welcoming him with open arms. Moreover, you shouldn't forget those who helped you at the beginning of your career.

French football's youth development system is said to be the best in the world, mainly because of the enthusiasm and discipline I've already mentioned in the academies. The coaches in charge are great tacticians and know so much about the game; that's why France's youth academies are world renowned. I never tried to get into the National Football Institute (INF). There are seven centres across France, at Castelmaurou, Châteauroux, Clairefontaine, La Madine, Lievin, Ploufragan and Vichy, set up by the French Football Federation (FFF). Generally, young players stay at the centres for two years (except at Clairefontaine, where they stay for three) before going on to complete their training with a professional club. They are said to be the best, and it's very difficult to get in.

While you shouldn't assume that all the best players go through the INF, obviously some great players have come out of these centres. When the cream of young French players are asked these days where they spend their formative years, they usually say the INF. Alongside them, each club is also producing future players, with three or four clubs standing out. Auxerre and Nantes, for example, have a reputation for producing good young players who are well trained by competent coaches. And, of course, there is Metz.

In my opinion the secret of the French system's success is its organisation. At the National Centre at Clairefontaine there's a library full of technical aides that coaches and teachers can draw on. Furthermore, our coaches have to attend well-structured courses to gain the necessary diploma, issued by the FFF, that entitles them to manage a team. Once they've qualified, they get to work within a long-established system in which young talent is quickly unearthed. That's also why French youth teams are so successful at international level.

Despite my success in the first team, at this stage I never contemplated being selected for the national team. Anyway, I wouldn't have fancied my chances of taking the place of an Eric Cantona or a Jean-Pierre Papin. Instead I was over the moon to be selected for the French youth team for the 1996 European Championships, and for the Olympic Games in Atlanta. We achieved quite a lot, but then we had a great team packed with talented players and hard workers.

Sometimes I talk to Sylvain Wiltord and Patrick Vieira about those days; almost all of that French youth side now play for big European clubs, and we owe a lot of that success to the grounding we had in the French system. It wasn't a bad side. Florian Maurice, Pierre-Yves André and Olivier Dacourt were all there, so it would be worth a few quid these days!

Then, at the end of the summer of 1996, and thanks to the progress I'd made at Metz, I was selected for the full France team. My wife, who was working for local radio, saw a press release announcing the squad and called me in the car. At first I thought it was a wind-up, but when I got home I turned on the telly and it was true.

My time at Metz was very important to me, both on a

professional and on a personal level – I met Nathalie while she was working at the Saint-Symphorien stadium. My only regret while I was at the club was that we missed out on the French league title in 1998 on goal difference. We ended up with 68 points, the same number as Lens, but lost the title because our goal difference was five goals worse off (+20 compared to +25). To have seen Metz as champions of France for the first time in their history would have been amazing. Personally, it would also have been a fitting way to end my time at the club. A few months later I signed for Olympique de Marseille, but I left Saint-Symphorien disappointed; even our League Cup final victory on penalties (5–4) over Lyon two years earlier couldn't make up for it. That afternoon at Parc des Princes was certainly a highlight, but it couldn't wipe out the bitter taste our failure to win the title left with me.

During that season when we came so close I began for the first time to feel the pressure of celebrity. It's one thing to dream of being famous and another actually to find yourself in a position where people recognise you when you walk down the street. For me that was very difficult, and I lost sight of when to say 'no' and when to say 'yes' to the various demands that were made of me. I was doing too much off the pitch and forgetting what I was there for.

It was just one of many different challenges I faced at Metz, from sitting on the bench in the early days, to being yelled at by Joël Muller during training, to the daily fierce competition with the other young players at the academy. But my heart is still maroon. I had set myself targets when I signed there and a number of people helped me achieve them: my parents, my trainers and managers, and not least my wife.

I'll never forget the people who have helped me wherever I go. I remember my friends in Reims calling me and saying, 'We thought that when you left you'd forget us.'

'You must be mad,' I replied. 'All right, today I'm on telly, I earn a lot of money, I'm in demand, but so what? You could say that if I hadn't known you, I wouldn't be where I am today.'

4

A Mess in Marseille

In December 1999, halfway through my second season in the south of France, Olympique de Marseille lost 5–1 at St Etienne. Our fans, understandably irate, took out their frustrations on the players, and in particular on our forward Christophe Dugarry. That night the atmosphere was explosive, hatred raining down on us from all sides. We were glad to get out of the ground, but when we got back to the team hotel the staff told us that we wouldn't be able to leave because some of our so-called 'supporters' were waiting for us in the hotel car park. We were trapped. With little option open to us, we were forced to stay the night and travel home the next day.

In the morning, the club officials told us that a meeting had been arranged between the leaders of the various supporters' groups and the players. Our coach at the time, Bernard Casoni, got six or seven of the senior players together and asked, 'Are any of you willing to go and talk to the fans?'

Deafening silence.

It was as if a school teacher had asked his class, 'Anyone fancy a detention?' We all avoided making eye contact with each other and no one dared raise his hand. Finally, the awkward fidgeting becoming unbearable, I volunteered. Why? Because I was the team captain and I felt it was my duty to go. Besides, I needed to know what the supporters wanted from us. My willingness encouraged some of the other lads to follow my lead, and we began preparing for the meeting fixed for the next day at our training camp at Commanderie. The trap had been set.

★

As a teenager I'd chosen to abandon my studies to play football. At the age of 24, and with my career blossoming at Metz, I was faced with another tricky decision. I'd made up my mind that it was time to move on and had actually been approached by Olympique de Marseille, AS Monaco and Paris Saint-Germain. In my eyes, Marseille were the biggest club of the three. Regardless of the fact that L'OM have struggled in recent seasons, they retain a certain cachet. They were the side of the 1980s when a team that included the likes of Jean-Pierre Papin, Basil Boli and Chris Waddle swept all before them in the French league and Europe. That period of unbridled success had ended abruptly when the club president Bernard Tapie was found guilty of bribing opponents. He was jailed, and L'OM had their French league title stripped and were relegated to the Second Division. But they had hauled themselves out of that spell in the wilderness, the former Millwall and Chelsea striker Tony Cascarino scoring a hatful at the lower level, and were back where they belonged, challenging for honours. My instinct told me this was the club to take me to the next level. Their size, their list of honours, their fanatic support, their history — all that attracted me to the Stade Vélodrome. I wanted this to be the next step in my personal adventure.

The coach Rolland Courbis and the club president Robert Louis-Dreyfus came to see me in Metz and said that I was the missing piece in their jigsaw. Their side was already nearing greatness, but I would complete it. As a sales pitch, that wasn't bad. Their enthusiasm was music to my ears, though my own advisers tried to dissuade me from going to Marseille. My mother wanted me to go to Monaco instead and my father was hardly convinced L'OM would be the best choice. He also preferred the idea of Monaco, as did Nathalie and Carlo Molinari, my chairman at Metz. Their reluctance was understandable. L'OM is synonymous with fervour, passion and excess, traits that don't necessarily smack of long-term security, and those close to me couldn't see beyond that. Still, whatever they told me about the city, about the club, I wanted to go there. In a way, the fact that I was going against the grain just made me feel even better.

I discussed the offer on the table from Marseille with Laurent Blanc and Christophe Dugarry who were already established in the team down there, and they encouraged me to come and join them. They said it would do me good and I'd enjoy it, but whatever advice you glean it always boils down to the player concerned whether he moves clubs or not. You can ask loads of people – parents, friends, agents – but you make the decision on your own – which explains why, against the wishes of my family, I opted to join Marseille.

My motivation wasn't financial. Mine was a sporting decision. I felt that signing for L'OM and playing alongside people like Blanc and Dugarry would benefit my career and help me progress. Lolo and Duga were leading lights in the France team, something I aspired to but was still a long way from achieving. Florian Maurice, then at PSG having just broken into the France side, had just decided to move to Marseille as well, which was another factor, but Courbis's side was packed full of experience. The goalkeepers Andreas Köpke and Stéphane Porato, the Italian forward Fabrizio Ravanelli and the defender Patrick Blondeau all gave the squad a powerful look which was supplemented by a clutch of talented youngsters – Peter Luccin from Bordeaux, Stéphane Dalmat from Lens – who had already been signed up.

Blanc was the most inspirational figure at the club. He was the leader, the player who best knew how to talk with the coach, the chairman or even the other lads. Every club needs someone like that, someone the younger players can lean on and turn to for advice. I would have loved to fill that role for Luccin or Dalmat, offering them advice, but I was not much older than either of them, so it was Lolo Blanc, Ravanelli and Köpke who took on that mantle. You couldn't help but listen when one of them had something to say because they'd all played at the highest level: Blanc had been with Barcelona in La Liga, Ravanelli with Juventus in Serie A and Köpke with Eintracht Frankfurt in the Bundesliga. They understood the pressures of playing for a massive club like L'OM; they were our big brothers in the camp.

Whenever you arrive at a new club you meet loads of players you've never heard of or met before, but although it had taken me time at Metz, I made a conscious effort to find friends on arriving at L'OM. I became good mates with the South African international Pierre Issa and Patrick Blondeau, both of whom played at Watford in the First Division during the 2001/02 season. It's always good to meet up with old friends in another country, and it happens quite a bit in football where you're constantly meeting new people and bumping into old team-mates.

The move from Metz to Marseille went through during the 1998 World Cup and actually constituted a record transfer between French clubs at the time, totalling some 60mFF (£6m). I only remember the figure because people still keep reminding me of it. 'Sixty million francs!' they marvel, as if I'd been the one carrying the briefcase stuffed full of 100FF notes. The size of the fee was nothing to do with me; that was down to the two clubs. The player doesn't touch any of that money. I knew that 60mFF was Carlo Molinari's asking price once he'd made it known he was willing to listen to offers for me, and that that was what Marseille were willing to pay. But I have to say it's an awful lot of money. It did cross my mind a few times whether I was actually worth that.

But, though the footballer doesn't see anything of the transfer fee, he does receive a 'signing-on fee' as a kind of incentive from his new club, and the fact that I was an international entitled me to a hefty amount. My agent proposed a sum to the L'OM chairman to kick off negotiations, with the eventual amount they settled upon coming straight to me. As well as this bonus, the footballer negotiates other aspects of the transfer along with his advisers, agents and lawyers. To that end, by agreeing to move from Metz to the south coast, the salary I hammered out with Marseille was eight times that I'd had at Saint-Symphorien.

It's hard to say whether I deserved that money or not, but the fact was that L'OM were willing to pay it. In any job, if you propose a salary to your boss and he or she comes back accepting the offer, you take it. That other people are jealous of what you can earn, or the life that a footballer leads, winds me up. We hear it all the time – 'Footballers are hideously overpaid' – but I'm sick and tired of that argument. Sure, we earn well, but compared to other sports our salaries are not that inflated, particularly when you compare them with Formula One racing drivers, tennis pros, golfers or NBA basketball players. Their wages, like ours, are only proportionate to the amount of money their sports generate. They are at the top of the game, the figures who attract the crowds and whip up the interest, so surely they should earn well.

You can't talk about professional football these days without mentioning the role of agents and the part they play in the structure of the game. As in anything else, there are good agents and there are bad agents out there, that's for sure. And I'm also certain that there are too many agents nowadays, many of whom have just jumped on the gravy train, lured in by the amount of money in the game. The good ones know football inside out, both on the pitch and behind the scenes, and have their client's best interests at heart. Agents pick up a commission on a player's transfer fee and too many just look to prompt as many big moves as possible, lining their own pockets in the process, rather than think about what's best for the player. We've got to clamp down on them, and that's why the authorities at national and international levels have attempted to regulate agents. They have to pass an exam now to become licensed agents. The tougher that test is, the better.

Agents are useful at certain points in your career, particularly when you're young and you need someone to give you a leg up into the big time. The best agents know how football works and understand the game, and they move in the same circles as the game's movers and shakers – the club chairmen or managers. These are the agents who can put a young player in contact with his first club. There aren't many professional players out there who don't have agents. Still, given time, a player gets to understand better the various clauses in a standard contract and can work out what he can and can't demand of his employers or potential employers. Indeed, I often ask myself whether an international footballer should really need an agent to look after him. By the time you're 27 or 28 and you've got the necessary experience behind you,

you should be capable of dealing with things like that yourself and going it alone.

But when I joined Marseille, my negotiating was done with the help of my agent Frédéric Dobrage, who used to deal with Jean-Pierre Papin and has worked more recently with Bixente Lizarazu. Nowadays I deal with the football side of my career myself, negotiating any contractual issues personally with my club, though I do have a lawyer who acts as my adviser and deals with things like merchandising, image and publishing contracts. You're courted quite a bit by the press and other brand names, but I usually listen to and then analyse the pros and cons of what they're offering with my adviser. I may also ask my family or team-mates for advice, but then I'll make my own decision. You have to stay on your toes all the time, particularly when you're talking to people because a chat with a stranger can quickly turn into a news story in the press. I prefer to remain discreet, to keep myself to myself. That's far safer.

While I feel competent enough not to require a football agent these days, I would say it's imperative that a lawyer reads over whatever contract has been offered. The most seemingly insignificant comma or full-stop can change the legal sense of a document, and I'm not capable of picking up on the small-print jargon, so I get my lawyer to go through any sponsorship contract I'm offered with a fine tooth-comb. When I changed my boot deal to Puma, my lawyer was the only intermediary between me and my new sponsor, and he did a similar job when I was thrashing out a deal to endorse Petrole-Hahn health products. Other footballers may act differently, with their agents out there peddling their names and attempting to attract sponsorship deals, but I wait until potential deals come to me. That's just the way I like it.

In truth, the main reason I ended up at Marseille was the enthusiasm of their coach, Rolland Courbis. He'd come and sought me out and gone out of his way to persuade me to join L'OM. I was to be his midfield fulcrum, he said, the central piece around which his team was to be built.

Rolland was an extravagant character who loved playing about with the team's tactics. You never quite knew what formation he was going to adopt next: we'd play with three defenders one week, then four the next and five the week after that. Rolland was always thinking up new tactics and strategies, which made it interesting if quite tough in terms of adapting. Footballers like to know exactly what is required of them and are more comfortable playing in a familiar style and formation every week, but that was Monsieur Courbis. You couldn't change the way he was.

At L'OM, he quickly had me playing in central midfield, a throwback to the role I'd played and enjoyed years before at Stade de Reims. I knew what it was all about – it was like going back to my roots – so I wasn't that thrown when the coach came up to me and explained that he wanted me in the centre playing just behind a front three. Indeed, for a year, the formation he adopted worked really well.

Rolland Courbis's faults as a man manager stemmed from his 'Southernness': he was impulsive and to the point, never shying away from speaking his mind, traits often associated with those from the south of France. In our second training session before the start of the 1998/99 season he drew up a list of players who were no longer part of his plans for the up-and-coming campaign. 'After today,' he told them in front of the whole squad, 'I won't need you any more and you are free to go and find yourselves new clubs.' Obviously that came as something of a shock for the lads on the list. On the eve of the new season these players were unceremoniously dumped in a very public way. It was pretty harsh, but at least he'd been frank and the players knew where they stood. If nothing else, he'd given those lads a chance to find a new club before the season began. Other coaches might have let them know only once the new campaign was underway, in which case it would have been far harder for them to sort themselves out with new clubs.

I got on well with Rolland, even if we were very different characters – he is the only manager, including Arsène Wenger, I've ever had who allowed me to call him *tu* rather than the more formal *vous* – but during my second season at the club he resigned, or was effectively pressured to do so, after a 5–1 Champions League defeat to Lazio. He was replaced by Bernard Casoni, a former Marseille player who knew the club inside out. It's always disruptive when the manager changes; you lose your bearings and have to adapt quickly to the style and tactics of your new boss. We all know it happens a lot in football and you just have to get on with your game regardless, but it seems to have become a habit for L'OM. It's the same in Italy where the managerial merry-go-round is as busy as the transfer market, but it's as if Marseille can only function with this constant cycle of instability. It's helpful if you understand that when you sign for them.

It could all have been so different. What with all the new faces, me included, Rolland had recruited that first season, we wanted to create a really tight-knit, warm feeling in our squad both on and off the field. We organised an afternoon's go-carting and a session at the local dry ski slope, just to get away from a footballing environment, as well as trips to restaurants with our wives and girlfriends.

Team spirit clearly benefited from this. One of our first games at the Stade Vélodrome was against Montpellier, and at half-time we found ourselves 4–0 down. That was a real slap in the face; even though it was right at the start of the season, we could feel the unrest sweeping through our supporters. But that day we were spurred on by the criticism and determined to come out in the second half and put things right. Florian Maurice quickly pulled one back, and Christophe Dugarry scored two more to make it 3–4. Then Eric Roy (who was to join Sunderland about a year later) equalised. Right at the death, I was fouled in the box and Laurent Blanc smacked home the penalty. We'd won 5–4. Those home fans who'd spent half-time moaning about us and our pathetic performance sat there in a trance. You only take part in a match like that once in your career, but that game set the tone for our season. It was a rollercoaster from start to finish, culminating in our appearance in the UEFA Cup final.

But it was the finale of our league campaign that lingers most with me. Going into the last weekend of the season we were second, a point behind the leaders Bordeaux. To have a chance of winning the title we had to win at Nantes and hope that Les Girondins did not do the same against PSG at Parc des Princes. Given the fierce rivalry between Paris and Marseille, it felt as if we might have missed our chance. It was hardly the ideal way for us to end our season, with the build-up dominated by rumours and counter-rumours that our bitter rivals from the capital might not try as hard as usual, just to make sure Bordeaux pipped us to the championship.

While I was not getting my hopes up that much, I still approached that final game of the season feeling that the championship was within reach, and when I opened the scoring against Nantes at Beaujoire I genuinely believed we'd be champions. All of us were aware that Bordeaux were level with PSG. We kept ourselves solid and held on to our narrow advantage, and after 85 minutes we heard that it was 2–2 at Parc des Princes. We were minutes away from winning it. Then, with two minutes to go, the news filtered through that Feindouno had scored a third for Bordeaux, effectively meaning the title was theirs and our dream, our whole season, was dead. All our effort had been for nothing. To have come so close was devastating both for the players and for the club, which hadn't won the title since 1992.

On a personal level, it would have been nice to have won it in my first year at the club, particularly after so many people had predicted I would fail if I went to Marseille. But it was all the more frustrating given that I'd just missed out at Metz as well, which left me feeling as if I was fated never to win the league. I don't want to question the validity of Feindouno's winning goal or take anything away from Bordeaux, who clearly deserved to win the title, but once again I'd been pipped to the post, and by a solitary point. Failure can help you develop as a player, teaching you to look to the future, look to the next time. Nevertheless, it was a massive setback, coming at the end of a season which had promised so much both in the league and in the UEFA Cup.

We had played some sparkling stuff to reach the final in that competition, knocking out some impressive sides like the Spaniards Celta Vigo en route. Not that it had all been plain sailing. The second leg of our semi-final took us to Bologna, the game finishing 1–1 which, thanks to the goalless draw we'd played out at our place in the first leg, was enough to take us through, but all hell broke loose on the final whistle. The atmosphere was spiteful, the red mist descending as players squared up to each other and to the police officers trying to escort us all off the pitch. I feared for my own safety and went straight back to the dressing rooms to wait for it all to calm down. Violent scenes like that are all the more shameful when they are actually provoked by the players themselves.

On the pitch, everyone loses his temper once in a while. It's difficult to keep yourself calm all the time, but you can't afford to let yourself be riled or provoked. I've fallen into that trap once or twice. When you're irritated – when you're losing, or when your opponent's winding you up – it's tempting to react, but it's at that point that you have to try to stay in control. If I'm being provoked by an opponent I prefer to respond with the ball at my feet, dribbling past him and leaving him for dead. Violence on the football pitch is no different from violence on the street, and anyone who resorts to it should be banned. Amateur footballers, particularly the young, watch games on the television and need to be set the right example.

We played Parma in the final, but we were without Dugarry and Luccin, both suspended after the events at Bologna, and also the injured Ravanelli and Roy. With a side decimated by their absence, we lost 3–0. That was a real disappointment. Everyone at L'OM dreamed of winning the trophy to make up for losing out on the championship, but we were beaten by a brilliant team that included my French team-mates Lilian Thuram and Alain Boghossian.

You have seasons like that. We lost out to Parma and Bordeaux, both of whom played their best football but were subsequently unable to live up to that level of performance. Neither club has won anything of note since, but they'd still managed to ensure that we had nothing to show from what should have been remembered as an excellent campaign.

In the summer of 1999 we went on a training camp to prepare for the new season. Our captain Laurent Blanc had just been sold to Inter Milan and Rolland Courbis came to see me. 'I'm thinking about making you team captain,' he said. 'What do you think?'

'Why not?' I replied. 'It would be an honour.'

I wanted to give him the impression that I wasn't over-awed by the prospect of taking the captain's armband, but I spent that pre-season fretting about the new role I'd be playing. As far as I was concerned, the team captain should be a leader, someone who feels happy communicating to the group. I wanted to give it a go, but in truth I had this nagging doubt that I wasn't up to it.

In hindsight, I now recognise that the captain's role at a club like Marseille was not meant for me. You have to have broader shoulders than mine to take it on, and I didn't have the extrovert personality needed. In that respect Patrick Blondeau was more suited to the job, and he took the armband after we lost 1–0 to Lens at home later that season. I know now that being captain involves a lot more effort and work than one may suspect, and I simply wasn't ready for it. I let things get to me, put myself under too much pressure and allowed what was going on around me to affect my game. If my club were to ask me to skipper the side now, I'd agree, but only because with the benefit of more experience I'd cope better now.

Initially, I hoped to impose a bit more discipline on the squad while still keeping the atmosphere as light-hearted as possible. To make sure all the players arrived for training on time, I introduced a fine system like the one we'd had at Metz with a fine of 10FF or 20FF for every minute you were late. I'd be there with the stopwatch, counting the squad in and adding up the fines owed, and the money soon piled up. I had to pay up myself a few times, but we raised enough for the squad to go out once in a while for a meal together.

That's all very well, but from the start things went badly on the pitch, which meant I effectively didn't have a chance. The results were awful. If the team had been playing as well as we had the previous season there wouldn't have been a problem and no one would ever have criticised me or my captaincy. But at Marseille I get the impression that the player wearing the captain's armband is the one who comes in for flak first. Lolo must have been able to take it; I was not.

I heard lots of people saying things about me, questioning whether I deserved to be captaining the side, commenting that I'd never really done anything at L'OM to justify that honour. It got to me quite a bit and I quickly worked out who I could trust and who I couldn't. People would tell me to my face that I was the best player in the side and the nicest person they'd ever met, only to stab me in the back as soon as the results started to go against us. When the team is not doing well, pressure tends to come in two forms: first of all the supporters get on your back and will let you know in whatever way they can that they are not happy with what's going on; then there's the press.

Journalists play an important part in football, which is why I always make a point of attending press conferences. These days, I talk to the media before and after games, and I'll travel back to Paris from London to be interviewed for television if necessary (I did that recently for a programme about Zinedine Zidane). It's hard for us to open the newspapers and read 'This bloke's no good' or 'He doesn't know what he's doing out there any more', but if a journalist writes something nice about you you're pleased enough. So when you're in a sticky patch you have to put up with the criticism – that's only fair.

At Marseille, we worked under pressure from the fans and the journalists all the time. The supporters demanded explanations for our poor performances, and so did the local, regional and national press. On top of the demands that were made on us by the press, the club had just set up its own in-house television channel, L'OM TV, with the players' wives asked to present programmes on air. Laetitia Roy and Eva Bravo, the wives of my team-mates Eric and Daniel, had already agreed to do just that. I spoke about it with Nathalie and explained to her that I wasn't really comfortable with it and didn't want to mix my professional and personal lives. She agreed, and did not take part, but the channel's very existence just added to the pressure. When things weren't going well on the pitch, it made life increasingly hard.

When you wear the blue and white of Marseille, you are representing more than a club; you carry the hopes of a whole city, its expectations and its fears, on your shoulders. The crowd at the Stade Vélodrome is one of the best you could play for, but it can also be one of the worst given the intense pressure they put you under. True to form, and with our results going from bad to worse on the pitch, there was a small but vocal minority who really kicked up during my time at the club.

I don't put all the Marseille fans in the same bracket; they are passionate and the majority just want the best for the team, and I got on well with them. Indeed, I even acted as an impromptu taxi service for some of them in my Polo. I'd leave Commanderie after training and head off towards Marseille to have lunch with my team-mates, and sometimes some of the fans would see me leave and ask if there was room in the car for them. I'd let them in and give a few of them a lift back into town. I got to know some of the fans that way, but then that's not saying much given that they'd turn up and watch us train. Commanderie was open nearly every day to the press and the public, so even the place where we were supposed to prepare ourselves in peace and quiet for games in the Champions League was laced with its own pressures on the players and the coaching staff, who seemed to be multiplying all the time. There were people hanging around who were supposed to be working with us, yet we had no idea what their function was. That didn't do much for team spirit either. While I like talking to the fans, I also need my own space to concentrate my mind and prepare myself for competitive action. At times, that was hard.

As that second season progressed, the relationship between the team and some of the so-called supporters became increasingly strained on the back of our sticky start. We didn't look like the same players compared to the previous season; our strikers weren't hitting the target, our defence was leaking goals left, right and centre and everything appeared to be falling to pieces. In team sports, whether amateur or professional, regional or international, you sometimes have seasons when everything just goes wrong. That seemed to be what was happening to us in 1999/2000. A year earlier we'd been fighting for the title; now we were struggling not to slip into the Second Division.

December was a terrible month for us, littered with sloppy displays and hardly a point to show for it all. Our nadir came with the defeat at St Etienne, the infamous 5–1 that lit the tinder. If we'd been teetering on the brink until then, that loss plunged us headlong into a full-scale crisis.

Reeling from that thrashing, we faced up to the meeting arranged with the leaders of the fan groups. We were aware of their disquiet, but we wanted to know what had driven them to barricade us into our hotel. The meeting was pretty pointless as we knew what they wanted – results – but we went along: me, the captain, Christophe Dugarry, Stéphane Porato, Florian Maurice, Frédéric Brando and Sébastien Pérez.

We arrived at Commanderie and immediately sensed that something was wrong. There was a poisonous atmosphere about the place. A small road led up from the centre's entrance to the pitches and the changing rooms, and as we drove through the gates in our cars the people gathered on the side of the road just glared at us. My instinct told me to chuck a U-turn and go straight home, but the meeting had been arranged and we had to see it through. I steeled myself and drove on.

But as soon as we reached the changing rooms and saw some 200 people waiting for us, it was clear this was an elaborate trap. We expected only the seven supporters' representatives to be up there, but the club had lied to us again. They hadn't kept us informed about the outcome of their discussions with the fans and had obviously held back crucial information. It was clear it was all going to kick off, but no security had been arranged for the meeting. The fans knew what was going on, but none of us did. The club just let us turn up and didn't even have the decency to warn us about what might happen. That sums them up.

We got out of our cars rather tentatively and the atmosphere suddenly grew extremely tense, especially when Dugarry emerged. The previous evening at St Etienne he had been roasted by some of the supporters. Thankfully, a few of the club's security guards emerged from nowhere to shield him, otherwise the situation might have really degenerated.

All six of us rushed into the changing rooms, and that's when it all went off. Outside, stones were hurled at our cars; Sébastien Pérez's windscreen exploded, and a smoke bomb smashed one of my windows. It was as if we were in Sarajevo with smoke billowing all around us. The whole place had gone mad. We were cut off in the dressing room and started to panic because we had no idea how this was going to turn out. The police turned up, but now the calls were repeated for us to come out and talk with the seven fans' reps. We didn't want to see anyone, we just wanted the situation to calm down, but that was not going to happen. The 'fans' only had one thing on their mind: to get into the dressing rooms and beat us up.

Eventually, the leaders of the seven supporters' groups battled through the pandemonium and reached the changing rooms, forcing their way in and shouting about how pissed off they were. Given the circumstances, that hardly came as much of a surprise. I got the impression that they were privately quite pleased that we'd been beaten 5–1 at St Etienne as it had given them the excuse to take out their frustrations in this violent way.

'All right, so you're not happy,' I replied. 'But do you really think we are either?'

At least after that we were finally able to open up some kind of reasonable discussion. We tried to explain to them that we hadn't enjoyed conceding five goals either and that we were trying our best for L'OM, even if we'd not been able to scale the heights of 1998/99. We reminded them that the team was different, that quite a few of last year's squad had moved on and been replaced by new players. Bit by bit, the tension dissipated, but we had to wait a long time for everything to calm down outside.

Some of the fans visibly regretted what was going on. Some of them had really wanted to talk to us and under-stand what wasn't clicking within the team and what could be done to put it right. Unfortunately, we only saw them well after the chaos outside had died down, and although we talked to them then, there were only a few left. Most of them had scarpered after we'd been ambushed by the yobs.

The whole thing was a hideous experience and many of

the players felt badly let down by the club, so much so that a few of them vowed never to play for L'OM again. I understood why they decided to leave. We'd paid the price for what football represents nowadays. Our fans had been whipped up by the excessive media coverage surrounding the club, enraged by what they deemed to be the overly large salaries we picked up. We paid because certain people were jealous of what we did and what we represented, and I'm not talking about the younger fans. The kids who watch us play dream to be just like us.

I understand the significance of a club to a region or a city, but the people who intimidated and attacked us that day had not dedicated their lives to football or tried themselves to become professional footballers. I followed my vocation in life, and no one was going to take that away from me, certainly not people who pretend to be football fans just so they can start a fight.

In January 2000, a fortnight after the events at St Etienne and Commanderie, I asked for a meeting with the chairman Robert Louis-Dreyfus, who was also the head of Adidas. He accepted, and we met in Adidas's head office in Paris.

'What can I do for you?' he asked before I'd even had a chance to sit down.

'Well, Mr Chairman,' I replied, 'I can't stay here. I have to leave the club.'

He was staggered, but at the same time seemed almost relieved. 'I had no idea you'd come here and tell me that,' he sighed.

'What did you think I wanted?'

'A pay rise, like all the others.'

Now it was my turn to be surprised. 'A pay rise?' I said. 'Now? You're mad. Haven't you seen how I've been playing? I'm all over the place. If you want to stop paying me at all, fair enough, but I'd prefer it if you'd just let me leave.' I wanted to go, nothing else. I needed to be released from my seven-year contract at L'OM and to leave at the end of the season.

Louis-Dreyfus thought for a while, eyeing me up and down and tutting under his breath, then gave me his response. 'Given the circumstances, I accept,' he said. 'You have my word: in June, I'll place you on the transfer list. Not before.'

I was relieved more than anything else. I told my parents, who were fretting about what was happening, that I'd be giving L'OM five more months of effort and that would be it. I'd be on my way. But those five months were going to be hard. I had to put to one side all the flak I was getting in the press over my indifferent form and to concentrate on L'OM's run-in to the end of the season. Euro 2000 was approaching and other opportunities were opening up for me – all that was exciting, but playing for a club you know you'll be leaving soon demands a certain single-mindedness. You still have to be professional, even if it's less about enjoyment; it's a matter of blocking out what's going on around you, getting your head down and giving your all.

I wanted to leave Marseille in the best possible position, certainly in the top flight. Relegation was unthinkable, and at least we succeeded in avoiding that. Every single one of the players wanted to leave the club, without exception, but we told ourselves, 'We're going to fight for this club for five more months. After that, we can leave with our heads held high.' In fact, those final few games did nothing to dampen my enthusiasm for or love of football.

We preserved L'OM's First Division status on the last day of the season by drawing 1–1 at Sedan. Nancy, who were the other club struggling to stay up, ended up slipping into the Second Division even though they finished with the same number of points as us. This time, for once, my team had the better goal difference. We'd avoided the drop by one goal.

I made a lot of good friends at Marseille and I give those that stayed at the club a call from time to time, just to see how things are going. I learned a lot at L'OM and my football continued to progress, but I also experienced the flipside. In the space of two seasons I'd gone from competing for the title and playing in the UEFA Cup final to struggling to avoid relegation. Some may say my stay in the Bouches-du-Rhône wasn't particularly memorable, but I don't regret going there. When things aren't going to plan, it toughens you up.

Olympique de Marseille has always had this pressure from outside and within, and the unstable, volatile everyday existence is part of what it is to play for them. It's that fiery reputation that gives the city and the club its character. As far as I'm concerned, they remain a massive club. Some people tried to ruin my time at the Vélodrome, but I still had some good times and met some genuine, appreciative supporters there. I haven't forgotten them and all those who helped me to see it through right to the end and did their best for the club. It was for those fans that we fought to stave off the drop, not for the morons who know nothing about football and made our lives hell.

5

The Arsenal Adventure

My first game for Arsenal was away from home at Sunderland in August 2000. The Stadium of Light was a fitting arena in which to start. It's a typically English ground where the home support bellow for their side from the first whistle to the last.

In the changing rooms before the match, Arsène Wenger read out his team for the game. I wasn't in the starting line-up. I didn't say anything. Having given his pre-match team talk, the manager came up to me. 'I've left you on the bench,' he said. 'I want you to watch how the game goes. I need you to understand how matches are played over here.'

I sat on the touchline and watched the game, but after about 25 minutes I was at a loss. I'd never seen such thunderous tackling, all studs up with arms flailing – how was I going to be able to make my mark in this type of football? This was some introduction to the English game; the ferocity out on the pitch and the passion in the stands took my breath away. Maybe I was better off staying on the bench.

I got on only near the end and we were beaten 1–0, the

match ending in furore with Patrick Vieira sent off and all sorts of accusations made about a scuffle in the tunnel involving Arsène. Even so, with the ground shaking from the pitch to the stands in that deafening cauldron of noise, I'd fallen in love with this vibrant style of football.

I'd always envisaged playing abroad once I reached my mid-twenties, and at 26 I was fortunate enough to do just that. While receiving my grounding in France, learning the basics, I didn't want to 'go into exile', so to speak, too early. That was why, when I had the chance to join Benfica, I turned it down. You see too many young players leaving to play abroad too early in their career and coming home, tails between their legs, just six months later. After Metz I'd wanted to go to Marseille, but the way I sketched out my career path was that eventually I would sign for a club outside France.

My transfer to Arsenal was less about the club's long-standing interest in signing me and more about my relationship with Arsène Wenger. It felt to me as though Arsène had been wooing me throughout my career. When I was playing for Metz in the mid-1990s, Arsène wanted me to join him at Monaco where I would have had to fight for a place in the first team with Thierry Henry, who was playing in my position on the left wing in those days. That actually dissuaded me from moving to Monte Carlo; having two left-sided midfielders at the same club didn't seem too clever and the transfer duly broke down. Strange that I should think that then, and then end up at Highbury playing alongside Thierry anyway!

At the end of my last season at Metz, in 1998, Monaco came back in for me but Arsène Wenger had left to manage Arsenal and the lure of Marseille was too much. However, in the meantime, Arsène had kept his eye on my progress. Just before Euro 2000, he found out that I'd asked to leave Marseille and he jumped at the chance to try to bring me to London. The problem was, Real Madrid had also enquired after me. Once again, it was up to me to make a difficult choice.

As far as my parents were concerned, they didn't mind which club I opted for, though after my experiences at L'OM my mother was secretly desperate for me to go to Arsenal. As a Spaniard, she thought the fervour and excess of Real would be too similar to Marseille. This time I decided to follow her instincts and chose to join Arsenal.

While I was with *Les Bleus* at Euro 2000 I spoke with Arsène Wenger on the phone every week because I needed to know how the possible transfer was progressing. 'My idea is to employ you in a new role back on the left side of midfield, like you played at Metz,' he told me, detailing the game-plan he hoped to implement. 'I want you to play to your qualities and rediscover your self-confidence. You've had a tough time at Marseille, but now you've got to free yourself.'

That really appealed to me, and I was keen to experience life in English football. Real still wanted me, but the wait was infuriating. Arsène had first to find out what was happening with Marc Overmars, the Dutch winger who was no longer in his plans and whom he was trying to sell. Marc was willing to leave, but was still sorting himself out, so I had to be patient until he, along with my France team-mate Emmanuel Petit, finally completed the move to Barcelona. While I was in limbo, Arsène stayed in constant dialogue with me, reassuring me and telling me, 'Don't worry, I'm still interested. I've made up my mind you'll be with us next season and I'm doing everything I can to make sure that happens.'

It's important to feel that a manager of the calibre of Arsène is behind you. To hear that you're really wanted gives you a real boost, and he was there at all the meetings I attended before putting pen to paper. I didn't actually meet any of the other Arsenal directors, or their vice-chairman David Dein, until I arrived at the club's London Colney training centre for the first time.

On Sunday, 2 July, France beat Italy 2–1 in the final of the European Championship. The victory came courtesy of Sylvain Wiltord's last-gasp equaliser and a golden goal from David Trézéguet, establishing us as European and World champions.

With that win still buzzing in my head, I travelled to sign my contract at Arsenal the next day. Early in the morning of 3 July a private aeroplane, sent by my new club, was waiting for me at Rotterdam airport. Once I'd arrived in England I underwent and passed the usual medical tests before signing the contract – it all went really quickly. That afternoon I was travelling back to Paris to rejoin my French team-mates to celebrate our European title. After all the interminable waiting I'd finally gone from being a Marseille player to being a Gunner almost in the blink of an eye. That Sunday and Monday were fantastic.

My thoughts, and my heart, were divided between the Gunners and *Les Bleus*. I left for Paris completely at ease; compared with Commanderie, I'd been struck by how wonderfully calm London Colney had been. At Arsenal it was clear that everything was geared towards allowing the team to prepare in the best way possible and the training camp was ideal, a long way out of town and slap bang in the middle of the countryside. While we train there are no journalists or supporters present. It's the ideal environment in which to work and is typical of the set-up at most English clubs. They go out of their way to look after their players and a lot of effort goes into making sure that we are not disturbed, even though it may not be the ideal situation for the supporters, who get to see their team only on a Saturday afternoon, even if they live with us, by proxy, every day of the week.

I'd whisper it at Highbury, but for any French footballer who finds himself playing in the Premiership, Eric Cantona is the inspiration. He was the first to succeed over here, winning over the fans at Old Trafford and inspiring the younger generation of English players, and any Frenchman following in his footsteps wants to do the same. The crowd at Manchester United still sings *La Marseillaise* in his honour; when I met him I felt like a little kid asking a star for his autograph.

I first saw Arsenal play on the television right at the end of the 1990s. I watched as Nicolas Anelka ('Nico'), Emmanuel Petit ('Manu'), Patrick Vieira ('Pat') and Thierry Henry ('Titi') exploded on to the English scene wearing the Arsenal shirt. Their success made me wonder, 'Why not me? Could that be me one day?' Football, especially at a professional level, is all about dreams, and it's great to look back now and see that that was one dream that came true for me. Even with the success I've subsequently achieved at Highbury, I haven't forgotten those days when I'd dream about playing in that team; when you see your friends and compatriots doing well, you want to share that success.

So, by 2000, I was a Gunner too. After my summer holidays I moved to London, initially lodging with Thierry Henry. I didn't know anything about the city other than what he'd told me, but the squad was to travel to Germany for pre-season training. On the day we were due to go the plan was to meet up at Highbury and, first thing in the morning, the club sent a driver to come and pick Titi and me up. We had a bit of time to spare before the group was due to leave, so Thierry offered to give me a quick tour of the stadium. Off we went, walking through the streets, until Thierry suddenly announced out of the blue, '*Voilà* Highbury!' I looked around, but all I could see were what appeared to be house fronts. I had no idea that behind these facades, which are actually classed as listed buildings, was a tightly packed, modern football ground. Indeed, my first reaction was to blurt out, 'You're not seriously telling me that that's your [yes, I said 'your' rather than 'our'] stadium?'

'Sure it is,' he replied, seeing my disappointment. 'I know it looks bigger on the telly. When I came here I expected a massive ground. Arsenal's a huge club, after all. Don't worry, when you run out on to the pitch for the first time and the fans sing your name, you'll feel as if there were 80,000 supporters in there.' In fact, Highbury can barely hold half that, but Titi was quite right. When you play there the atmosphere is amazing.

I seemed to fit into the team pretty well straight away and was given the nickname D'Artagnan, courtesy of my beard. It was Nicolas Anelka who thought I ought to grow a goatee just before the Euro 2000 final. 'It's time you had a new style,' he told me. 'You should grow a beard between your chin and your mouth, forget the moustache. That would look good on you.' I took his advice, thought it looked good and kept it. It was only when the Arsenal captain Tony Adams saw it that D'Artagnan's name cropped up. It made me chuckle, hearing him pronounce it with his broad London accent, but from then on I became the Gunners' very own musketeer.

What Adams said pretty much went. He's a great man and was a great player who'd endured a torrid time in his personal life, what with his health problems and going public with his alcoholism, but he beat it and chose to write an amazing book about it. He's come a long way since them. Everyone always talks about the French players whose careers have taken off under Arsène, but Tony also had good reason to thank him. Arsène Wenger helped him rediscover his enthusiasm to play, as well as his best form out on the pitch. He was an inspirational figure; his relationship with the club was one that every footballer can envy. He started and finished his career at Highbury, his loyalty and love for the club unquestionable. Theirs was a rare and magnificent marriage.

His retirement in the summer of 2002 left a void. You don't play for a club for almost 20 years without making your mark, without creating your own legend, and Tony did that. Replacing him would be impossible, as I cheekily told Pascal Cygan when he was signed from Lille that summer. His arrival bolstered our ranks and ensured we had a left-footed defender competing for Tony's central place along with Martin Keown, Sol Campbell, Matthew Upson and Igor Stepanovs.

All of them are, in their own right, marvellous defenders: Pascal is quietly driven; Martin is all homespun spirit; Sol is a defensive monster whom I'd hate to be faced with as an attacker; Matthew is young and will be great; Igor is so calm. Add to those five our full-backs starting with Ashley Cole, one of the most natural English talents playing in the Premiership, and you begin to understand why this team has the makings of greatness. When I came to the club they still boasted the majority of the members of their trademark back four, the defence that had become synonymous with all things 'Arsenal' with the huge presence of Tony, our goalkeeper David Seaman and Lee Dixon, as influential in the changing rooms as he was at right-back. It's a shame I never got to play with Nigel Winterburn and Steve Bould as well, but I know how much the club owes them. Much of our success these days was built on that solid back-line.

★

Moving to another country is a complicated process, and not only because of all the bureaucratic paperwork you have to fill in. When you leave a French club to play for a foreign team, life changes. Of course, it didn't help that I didn't speak great English. The season after I joined, I was named Man of the Match after a game against Aston Villa and had to go in front of the television cameras to accept the award. I turned to David Seaman and spluttered in broken English, 'He speak, me *non*.'

Football was invented in England, and when you come here to play it's important to show that you want to be integrated into that grand tradition. The clubs and fans go out of their way to welcome you and adopt you as one of their own – look at how the French players have been accepted at Arsenal – and we, in turn, have a duty to immerse ourselves in this footballing culture. I like England, despite the problems I've had with getting used to the food and driving on the other side of the road. There's always a transitional period during which you have to adapt to everyday life in a new country, and I can understand better now why some French players fail abroad and quickly end up going home. It's hard to throw yourself into new surroundings when you've also got to concentrate on your game.

Finding somewhere to live is your first problem. No one at the club helped me to find a house in London, which was good in as much as it made me stand on my own two feet. You need to find a flat where you feel at ease, and I initially chose a spot in Soho, right in the centre of the city, that suited me. But after a few months my wife and I eventually opted for a flat near Regent's Park, a bit further north.

Getting to training every morning wasn't easy for me, so at first, as I said, I lodged with Thierry Henry. We didn't know each other that well before I arrived, but the fact that I lived with him for a month helped us become firm friends. He took me everywhere, not just to training but on guided tours too, and basically got me out and about in London. Then, when Nathalie was involved in a serious car crash in Canada and couldn't travel to join me immediately while she recuperated, I stayed in a hotel in Swiss Cottage for five months. Sylvain Wiltord was staying on the same floor and I'd known him for quite a long time having played with him for France, particularly with the under-20s. We're very close. If my wife was using the car and I needed to get to the stadium, Sylvain would lend me his without a second thought.

You spend a lot of time in hotels immediately after being transferred, but also during the season on the night before away games. We sometimes stay the night after as well if we're playing a game too far away from home to go straight back. It's the same with the France team – we're forever finding ourselves cooped up in hotel rooms. Time always passes slowly because you don't feel at home, stuck in unfamiliar surroundings. I hadn't ever lived in a hotel before I came to London, and it's an experience I wouldn't be too keen to repeat. It amazes me that some players actually prefer to live in hotels all year, as do some coaches like Rolland Courbis.

While I tried to get my bearings in London, I also had to make my mark out on the pitch. Trying to impose yourself at a big club where virtually every player is an international is a real battle. If I've done well in England, both on the pitch and off it, I owe a lot to my compatriots at the club. We have generated a kind of 'French solidarity', which is just as well given that I arrived in a foreign country, hardly spoke a word of the language and would have been completely lost without them. Each of them helped me in one way or another; Patrick Vieira and Gilles Grimandi also gave me some advice as to where to live.

And throughout this settling-in period I had the full support of Arsène Wenger. It's not hard to say good things about someone like Arsène. You only have to see what he achieved at Monaco, where he won the French title, the French Cup and took them to the European Cup Winners' Cup final. And then in Japan at Nagoya Grampus Eight he won the J-League and the Emperor's Cup in 1995. Add to that the Doubles he's claimed at Highbury in 1998 and 2002 and his qualities are obvious. Wherever Arsène goes he succeeds. He lives for football; it courses through his veins.

It was odd for me when I first arrived to find he was addressed as 'coach' because the equivalent word in French, *l'entraîneur*, does not carry the same weight. I now understand that it is a mark of respect and one that he very much deserves. The most remarkable thing about him is his ability to bring the best out of a player, forever making sure he feels completely at ease with his surroundings. He tries to make us understand how football works, and when he explains things the game seems so easy. He doesn't want our heads crammed full of tactics, he just wants us to keep things simple.

By the middle of the season, training becomes more about maintaining physical condition and maybe fine-tuning tactics and less about basic technical work, mainly because the games are coming thick and fast. We have to play every three days or so, so Arsène makes us follow a clear set of routines that allow our bodies to recover from the last game and prepare for the next as quickly as possible. I know he loves the tactical side of the game: the day before a match he'll make us work on set-pieces and corners, but he won't make us sit down and analyse our opponents' tactics. He'd rather we worked on our own game, which is one of the reasons why, when we do what the manager says, we are able to impose ourselves and play to our strengths. Every team has a way of playing, its own set tactics. Clearly, we like to play a traditional 4–4–2 and then tweak certain aspects to make the difference in competitive action, like working on how to defend free-kicks.

When I arrived at the club, Arsène took time out to talk to me as much as he could. It was almost as if he was looking out for me, perhaps because he'd heard that some people had taken advantage of me at Marseille, hanging around the club captain for their own good and not mine. Arsène does it for everyone, though. He'll talk to you a lot when you first join the club, or whenever he feels you're off your game, cajoling you until you're back to your best again out on the pitch. When he senses you're at ease, he'll simply let you be. He doesn't tell you how well you're playing; players know when they're on form, and Arsène just leaves that to you to work out for yourself.

English players never let up, running themselves into the ground for 90 minutes. I didn't have that mental and physical aggression when I initially arrived. The first quality would come with time, but I could do something about the physical side immediately. When I arrived after Euro 2000, Arsène wanted me to work on my upper body strength because he realised I was too frail for the Premiership. With the help of Arsenal's physical trainer, I was given a personal programme which I followed religiously, never exceeding the amount of muscle work I was supposed to be doing but never shirking from it either. All that hard effort in the gym at London Colney turned out to be very useful, making me stronger on my feet so that I was better able to hold off tackles from opposing defenders. That side of English football is great, even for a player like me whose game is more technical than physical.

When it comes to physical fitness work or weight-training I've heard that some players, particularly in Italy, take on such heavy workloads that they become physically ill, sometimes prompting them even to vomit. What good can that do? Each player should have his own programme geared specifically to his needs. Every footballer is different, with some more solid than others and some stronger technically. An individual set of exercises is a must. To that end, and in addition to the physical programme he draws up, Arsène also implements specific training plans for each of his players. At the beginning of the season he'll divide the squad into groups, basically the strongest and the weakest. Within each of these groups, each player can work at his own pace – whether it be for shooting, dribbling, sprints or long-distance runs – going quicker or slower depending on what works for him.

In my case, Arsène wanted me to rediscover the confidence I'd lost at Marseille. He emphasised the basics of my game and sharpened my natural instincts; he wanted me to pick up the ball and run at my opponents, taking them on. It was the type of thing I did all the time in training, so he worked with me on my dribbling, giving me the confidence to take these skills back out on to the pitch proper. It may sound odd, but we tend to try to improve what are deemed to be our best qualities. For example, Thierry Henry works a lot on his pace and I'll concentrate on my ball skills. It clearly does the trick.

Competition brings out the passionate side of Arsène Wenger's nature. His pre-match talk lasts seven minutes – any longer and he reckons it would be counter-productive. That may shock those who think a tactical genius should speak for a long time, explaining the complexities of what he wants done, but Arsène keeps things short and sweet. He briefly uses the blackboard in the dressing room to remind us of the specific things he wants each of us to do: he

underlines the strong points on which our defence and
attack should lean, what we should be doing at corners,
who should take free-kicks and penalties. It's all very
compressed and to the point. For him, football has to be a
game everyone can understand.

Every coach has a different idea of 'perfection', but the
master tactician in my opinion is the one who hands the
responsibility over to the players. When a club manager
has players of the calibre of Marcel Desailly (the France
captain and Chelsea defender) from whom to choose,
there's not much he can tell them that they don't already
know. The player knows what he has to do, and it's the
same for us at Arsenal. A lot of us are between 28 and 33,
so we know what is at stake in every match and what is
expected of us.

I've only ever once seen Arsène flustered or annoyed,
when we lost 6–1 at Manchester United in March 2001.
But that was understandable given that we had conceded
five goals by half-time against the team we were chasing in
the title race. In the changing rooms at Old Trafford Arsène
rightly went berserk, but his footballing philosophy stayed
the same. Out on the pitch there's not much point in
complicating life. He taught me that, and ever since I've felt
much freer whenever I've played.

Losing so badly to United that time really hurt us. Over
the last few years we have been competing with Sir Alex
Ferguson's side for honours – when Liverpool finished
second in 2002 it was the first time any other side had ended
up in the top two since 1997 – and we do hold them in high

respect. But it's not as if we are completely overawed by their recent achievements. We'd prefer to concentrate on our own qualities rather than marvel at theirs; we don't stick one finger up at them, but we don't fear them either. They have some great players in their ranks. Paul Scholes is my favourite. He's always available, demanding the ball; he takes risks, but he knows how to defend, how to mark, how to wriggle through a congested midfield and dictate play. He is a quality player. People talk about Roy Keane, and David Beckham grabs most of the headlines, but I reckon Scholes is integral to United's success. Invariably, if he's on form, so are United. It's the same with England as well. When he was slightly off colour at the World Cup, Sven Goran Eriksson's side did not pose the same threat.

But United have other things going for them as well, not least Old Trafford itself. It's the most awe-inspiring stadium in Europe, much better than those Italian grounds like the Olympic Stadium in Rome. A lot of people criticise the atmosphere on a matchday there, but as far as I'm concerned it takes the breath away. It can be very intimidating, particularly when they score. I remember going there with L'OM in a Champions League group match, and when they equalised I thought the stadium had exploded. The noise was terrifying. That shook us all up, and within ten minutes they'd turned it around and won 2–1. That tends to happen up there – if they score once, they're likely to add another quickly afterwards because the momentum carries them forward. United may be a great side, but with their vociferous support urging them on they're something else.

That said, the best fans in the world are still the Gooners who'll back us whether we're attacking or defending.

Arsène's encouragement eventually helped perk up my form, though I found it hard to stamp my authority on games until I'd chalked up my first goal for the club. That came in October 200 in the Champions League at Lazio, an equaliser that ultimately saw us qualify for the second phase of the competition for the first time in the club's history.

That goal came as a double relief. I'd been in the Marseille side that was thrashed 5–1 in that stadium a year earlier, a defeat that cost Rolland Courbis his job, so this was a chance for revenge. I was desperate to do well, but we found ourselves a goal down and, given my indifferent form, I just couldn't see myself scoring. Then, out of nowhere and with only two minutes to go, I produced the goods. I picked up possession on the left, cut inside and drilled a low shot beyond Angelo Peruzzi. Seeing the ball nestling in the back of the net came as a hell of a relief. I could hardly remember the last time I'd scored it had been so long, but from nothing I'd broken my duck and played my part in qualification. The sense of relief was amazing.

The goal was probably the key moment in my first season at Arsenal. I'd struggled during my first few months at the club, even if in hindsight I can still draw positives from that difficult start. I'd been thrown into English football and had grappled with the physical side of the game. Matches would pass me by. I just couldn't get a grip on games and make a proper impact. Perhaps the size of the £6m transfer fee was weighing on my shoulders more than it had at Marseille, but I wasn't living up to my billing. At times it did cross my mind whether I'd made the right decision coming to England. After my tricky last season in Marseille, it had been a long time since I'd been completely happy with my game. I certainly felt that there were some doubters even among the Arsenal supporters while I struggled on the pitch. Thankfully, the other French players and the manager kept geeing me up, telling me I'd get used to it, and their words of encouragement eventually paid off.

In truth, things weren't going well with the whole team either. At the midway point in the 2000/01 season, United led us by 11 points at the top of the table. Even at that stage, clawing that margin back was always going to be virtually impossible, not that our team spirit was damaged by the deficit. For that game in Rome our goalkeeper was the veteran John Lukic, who played while David Seaman was recovering from injury. As our third-choice goalkeeper he hadn't played a competitive game for three years, but he came in, kept the dressing room buzzing before kick-off and then had a brilliant game. We would have been dead and buried by Lazio well before my late equaliser if it hadn't been for his performance.

That's typical of the English mentality. It's all about respect. I remember when Rémi Garde, the first of the French players to come to Arsenal and now an expert analyser on French television's football coverage, came back to Highbury to cover a game. All the players bar none took time out to have a chat with him and wish him well. That just sums it up, the Arsenal spirit.

Things improved steadily for me after the Lazio goal, but an end-of-term report after my first season would still have read 'Must try harder.' It's safe to say life wasn't always rosy that year and, as I mentioned earlier, I let the frustration get to me at times. I've only been wound up twice since I came to play in the Premiership, and the first time was during that first year in a League game at Elland Road where I allowed myself to get totally carried away. David O'Leary, the former Arsenal defender and the Leeds manager at the time, was giving it plenty from the touchline during the game and calling me this and that, mainly because his team were winning 1–0 and he was desperate for the final whistle. I'm not a whinger and I wouldn't normally react, but the fact that the opposing coach was giving me so much grief really got to me. What kind of example was he trying to set for his players? As we returned to the dressing rooms at the end, we had a go at each other. The red mist descended and the insults flew. I wasn't thinking about what I was saying, I was livid. Stupidly, I even tried to punch through one of the windows. At least I pulled myself together in time.

The second time was during 2001/02 up at St James's Park after we'd drawn 1–1 in the FA Cup. I squared up to Jamie McClen during the match and went face to face with the Newcastle coach John Carver in the tunnel afterwards. Once again, words were exchanged and they weren't particularly polite. But I do try not to let myself get fired up when opponents start having a go. I remember playing against Chelsea's Dennis Wise (surprise, surprise) and almost losing my head, but you have to remind yourself that that's how some of these people operate. It's part of their tactics and you have to try not to let them win. Wimbledon kept themselves in the Premiership for years going out of their way to unsettle opponents in whatever way they could; Wise must have learned how to do it while he was at Plough Lane. It's something you just have to deal with.

Thankfully, I'm much better at expressing myself with the ball at my feet out on the pitch. That's where I can make my presence felt, and increasingly my team-mates and our supporters expect me to take the game by the scruff of the neck. That's a nice feeling; it's a feeling of responsibility, and I'm sure it helps me to raise my game.

As it was, we ended the 2000/01 season well behind United in the League and beaten in the FA Cup final by Liverpool. We dominated that match in Cardiff, led through Freddie Ljungberg but left with nothing courtesy of a two-goal mugging by Michael Owen. That summed it up. We'd been the better side that day, but had missed our chances. Personally, I'd missed an opportunity to stamp my authority on the English game that season, but maybe that defeat in Wales steeled the whole team's resolve to do better the following year. I was desperate for the new season to start so I might show the Highbury fans what I could really do.

I did just that. The injury aside, my second season in England couldn't have been more perfect and culminated in my first domestic League title, with the FA Cup, lost so cruelly a year earlier, thrown in as well. The day we celebrated our Double at Highbury will stay with me for the rest of my life: 11 May 2002, the festivities pre-empted by a 4–3 victory over Everton. The cup had been won with a 2–0 victory over Chelsea in Cardiff a week before, and the League title had been claimed at Old Trafford of all places three days earlier. That Saturday afternoon it was as if I was the star attraction, if only because I was the last player before Arsène Wenger to lift the trophy. Everyone in the ground seemed to be chanting my name. This was why I had chosen to come to Highbury rather than go to Real Madrid; it was as if this club was a little pocket of paradise.

Those were the first trophies I had won with Arsenal, but I was just as chuffed to have established myself at last in the first team prior to my injury. We might not have done as well in Europe as we'd have liked, but I'd played in all the Champions League games and, right through to January and February when I'd first started to feel tired, I'd played at my best in the Premiership too. After all the self-doubt during my first year at the club, I had hoisted my game to another level. I hadn't been injured or suspended. Some people urged me to take my foot off the pedal and avoid burn-out, but I went for every game. That's the way I am, and I'm pretty sure my commitment was appreciated by the fans who watched me every week.

In truth, the way the club goes out of its way to help players settle and concentrate on their game was bound to rub off on my form eventually. I heard a lot about the traditions in English football before I arrived, some of which – including the boot cleaning one – I thought could not be true. But when I arrived at Highbury I saw it for real.

Discipline plays a big part in English clubs, and at the majority of them the youth-team players still clean the professionals' boots. They pick them up after training or matches and bring them back as good as new – it's the rule, but there's a logic behind it. It's a kind of rite of passage for the apprentices en route to becoming professionals, the notion of respect for the senior players at its core. But at the same time the junior members of the squad still have a chance to play. The manager, when he makes his team selections, isn't influenced by players' names or reputations but by their form.

At Arsenal we are really pampered. Two club employees, a 'father' and his 'son', are assigned to each player. They hang our shirts up in the changing rooms at Highbury, always on the same peg in our designated place. It's the same at the training ground, where our shorts, socks, training shirts, bibs, towels and even swimming trunks in case we want to go for a dip are laid out by our lockers by the time we arrive. Everything's put on a plate for us. I still find the fact that someone else cleans our boots rather odd though, given that our boots are effectively the tools of our trade. In any other profession, you'd never want to let them out of your sight. But this 'father and son' duo accept and like their work and prefer it if we just let them get on with it. If we try to stop them they object, saying, 'No, let us do that. We're paid to do this.' So when we finish training we give them our boots, and when we come out of the shower there they are, waiting for us. I don't think I'll ever get used to it. It reminds me of what my mother used to do for me when I was young: she'd help pack my bag for me and then take my dirty kit away after training. At Arsenal it's as if I'm returning to my childhood: everything is done for me and I don't have anything to do other than play football.

When I'm out on the pitch I only have one thing on my mind – to win. If things don't go the way I'd like, at least I know I have an opportunity to put things right a few days later when, more often than not, we have another game. We play that much. I always want to win, but I've also learned to put things into perspective: compared with lots of things that happen in the world, miscontrolling a pass, missing a chance or even losing a game really isn't that important.

Footballers have a reputation for being superstitious, and a lot of us are. When I started out I had certain habits I stuck to. At Metz I always wore the same clothes on a matchday, the same shinpads, the same underpants, the same towel, but that's been drummed out of me at Arsenal. How can you stick to the same 'lucky clothes' if you are presented with spanking new kit for every match?

But those little details, designed to allow the team to prepare in the best conditions really do help and contribute to the relaxed atmosphere that's always there whether it be before a Premiership, a Champions League or a friendly fixture. English players are far more relaxed than players on the continent. At Arsenal the lads are still joking and having fun even a few minutes before kick-off, and you can bet there'll be music playing in the dressing room. I know that when the first French players came to the club – Patrick Vieira and Rémi Garde back in 1996 – they'd play techno music before matches. Nowadays, no doubt down to the French influence, there's more R&B and hip-hop. Anyone can put on a CD, but if the others disagree with the disc-jockey's choice he's shouted down and banned from putting any more on in future. And all the time, Arsène Wenger never interferes. I'm always surprised to see him chuckling when he hears some of our choices, which would hardly be his cup of tea. But they get us going, just as that song 'Jump' by Van Halen used to at Marseille when they played it at the Stade Vélodrome as the teams ran out.

Obviously all clubs have their own little idiosyncrasies, but by and large a footballer's everyday life is pretty much structured the same way wherever you go. At Arsenal we arrive at London Colney, half an hour's drive from the centre of town, at 10.30 in the morning for training at 11. Once changed, we have about ten minutes to get on to the pitch and make sure we don't get fined for being late. Training will last between 75 and 90 minutes, after which we can get a massage, go for a swim or use the jacuzzi or steam room. We're spoiled for choice. At about one o'clock we can go upstairs for lunch – it's not compulsory, but the majority of the players tend to eat there because there's a decent atmosphere and the food's good. They serve plenty of vegetables, starchy foods, meats and fish. The club doesn't have a nutritionist and none of the players feels it is necessary to consult one. I eat plenty of starchy foods and fish so I don't take any supplementary vitamins or energy pills. French meals may be more balanced nutritionally than those in England, but there are still plenty of products and restaurants here designed for top-class sportsmen. The other French players at the club and I have become regulars at certain restaurants: Base in Hampstead, where you can people-watch to your heart's content, or the Moroccan café Momo's in Soho. We'll go for the more exotic dishes, but never to excess. On a day without a game we leave London Colney after training to rejoin our wives and partners at home. Recuperation is key if you're going to perform at your best, so a siesta allows the body to relax and store up energy ahead of games.

There's a different drill on matchdays. The day before a home game we meet up at Highbury at about six o'clock in the evening, leaving our cars at the car park there before taking a coach to a hotel for the night. We eat and then spend the evening together, playing cards or napping, drinking coffee or tea at the bar and chatting among ourselves. The next morning we're up by about 9.30, go for a stroll outside together at around 10 and then have lunch before the manager gives us a short pre-match team talk. We leave for the ground well before the three o'clock kick-off. Even for home fixtures, those overnight stopovers are important and help to harness team spirit. By the time we're in the dressing room with the music blaring it can be difficult to concentrate, but there's never any pressure on our shoulders. We tell ourselves we're going to go out there and win; that's what is expected of us and that's what we're intent on doing.

On the personal side, my decision to sign with Arsène has proved to be a good one. By coming here I

I feel part of the London scene, where I can walk the streets without being pestered by autograph hunters. That's a refreshing change after Marseille, and I can thank the local lads – like Sol Campbell – for helping me settle in so quickly here.

While my France team-mates were struggling to defend the World Cup in South Korea, I spent the summer of 2002 on the French Riviera working with Tiburce Darrou in a bid to strengthen up my right knee. I have never worked so hard in my life.

Arsène Wenger would telephone me every morning during my rehabilitation in France to check how I was doing; that I was working seriously and was focused on returning. Once I was back at London Colney he took me under his wing and guided me through the last few months until my return. He is an inspirational coach, a man of true quality.

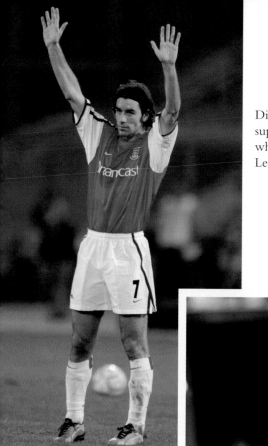

Disappointed but thanking the Arsenal supporters who had travelled to Turin for what proved to be our last Champions League game of the 2001/02 campaign.

Receiving the English Football Writer's Player of the Year Award. A proud moment.

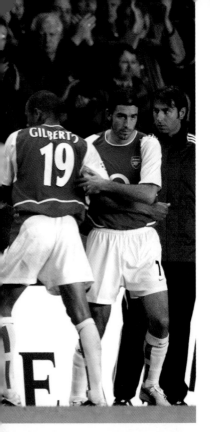

(*Left*) I had waited six months for this day, but to run on to the Highbury turf as a substitute for Gilberto Silva was a wonderful feeling. The reception the Arsenal fans gave me that evening will stay with me for the rest of my life. (*Below*) After Auxerre, Blackburn and Dortmund, I finally had a goal to celebrate in the Worthington Cup defeat to Sunderland. Scoring always gives you a buzz, but after such a long absence this was something special.

Celebrating my goal against Sunderland with Giovanni van Bronckhorst. My Dutch team-mate was also marking his return after long-term knee problems – together, it was good to be back.

experienced a new country, a new mentality, a new way to prepare myself for a game and, above all, a new town. London's a cosmopolitan city where you can walk down the street and not attract much attention, which is an incredible bonus for me. I can go shopping with my wife without being bothered by autograph hunters. Most people can take that for granted, but that isn't always the case for footballers. I can even go and eat at a restaurant (I'd stay incognito if I went clubbing!) or for a stroll down the road without people stopping and pointing. Then again, we don't get that much time to go out; what time we do have we spend with our families, or relaxing. Even in London, where everything's open seven days a week, 24 hours a day, I don't have enough time to go to the cinema or the theatre. That's why when I go back to France I'll try to do anything other than play football. Even so, I do appreciate living in London. Indeed, it seems like a paradise compared with my difficult last seven months in Marseille. I love the city and I've never felt threatened here. I feel as if I'm just like everyone else and don't stand out at all, which is great. People don't recognise me but they respect me; that's rarely the case in France, especially in Marseille where I was followed night and day by a media circus.

There may be around ten different League clubs in London, but of course it's the games against our neighbours Tottenham Hotspur that really matter. I'd heard about the traditional rivalry between the two clubs before I arrived, but nothing prepared me for the reality. When I scored the winner against them in the semi-final of the FA Cup towards the end of my first season at the club, I was blown away by the crowd's reaction. It was a precious goal that took us into the final and it was a great moment for me. Even if I end my career back in France, the din from the Gooners when that goal flew in will stay with me. It's something I'll remember for the rest of my life.

In recent years, Chelsea have emerged as challengers in the city as well, prompting Arsène Wenger to insist publicly on numerous occasions that it's harder for London teams to win the League because every other week throws up another derby game. Clubs elsewhere don't really have that problem, so the boss has got a point. Our matches with Chelsea have taken on added spice in the last few years because they've always been competing at the top as well, though they're invariably just behind us in the pecking order. To see people like Deschamps, Leboeuf, Desailly, William Gallas and, from 2001, Emmanuel Petit in their ranks just added to the occasion, and I've always been wary of the skills of Gianfranco Zola. He's a real jack-in-a-box. He may be small, but he's a genius out on the pitch and proved as much with his blistering start to the 2002/03 season.

The passion for football in England still takes my breath away. It doesn't matter what time of day you turn on the television, there's invariably a game on from either the Premiership, the Nationwide League or one of the cup competitions. And the stadia are always full. I remember tuning in one evening, watching a First Division game from

Hillsborough and seeing the stands jam packed. That wouldn't happen in France.

Foreign players have to adjust to the fact that there are games at strange times throughout the week — Monday night, Sunday lunchtime — and throughout the year. They take place over Easter weekend and at New Year, which does not happen on the continent. I do my best every game, telling myself that playing at such unusual times allows more people to get to the match. We play three times between Christmas and New Year's Day, and some of the lads don't like that, but I feel lucky to have the chance. They're traditional games over here with the grounds crammed full of people on holiday who have come with their families to watch us play.

A player's relationship with the fans is crucial, as had been proved to me powerfully at Marseille, and at London Colney the staff are always laying out posters, postcards and shirts for us to sign for anyone who asks for one. A lot of them are auctioned off by charities, but we have a responsibility when it comes to the fans. I try to reply to all the letters that are addressed to me, even if I still have trouble reading English. At L'OM I used to get a sackful of fan mail, some of which was forwarded from my fan club at Metz. They'd put all the letters in a huge plastic bag — not to chuck them away but to make them easier to carry — and I'd reply to them all. If people are out there thinking about you and taking the trouble to write, it's your duty to write back. I'd send a signed photograph, or a signed team photo, which was what most of the fans wanted. It's always nice to receive letters and good luck messages, though at Marseille I was a bit overwhelmed by it all and had to ask the fans to supply stamped addressed envelopes if they wanted me to write back. It wasn't a question of money, but time. In the same way, I've learned to carry on walking when I'm signing autographs. If you stop to sign them, you can be there for ever!

Every goal you score is significant, never mind who you are, what level you're playing at or which division you're in. Even more so when, like me, you don't score that often. But a goal is also an opportunity to be united with the fans. Just before I suffered my knee injury in mid-March 2002 I scored a beautiful and significant goal at Aston Villa that helped win us the match and took us top of the table. My immediate reaction was to go over to our fans, who were packed into one corner of the ground near the goal into which I'd scored. I stood there in front of the away supporters, watching them and sharing the moment. They give everything to follow us up and down the country, forking out for travel and match tickets. The least you can do is turn to them after a goal before celebrating and hugging your team-mates.

Of all the players who have helped me at Arsenal, none has been more significant than Patrick Vieira. He has become our on-field inspiration and has steadily taken on more and more responsibility at the club to become a huge figure within the squad. I think he's learned a lot from Tony Adams; last season he wore the armband whenever Tony was absent. He made sure we didn't miss Tony's leadership by being so authoritative in his play and demeanour, and now he has been made captain permanently we can expect more of the same. He takes his role as a leader very seriously, and in turn he is adored by the Highbury faithful. He has become an Arsenal idol and a legend in our half of north London.

He talks to me a lot as well, telling me how I should play and how, above all else, he likes me to come back and defend. My game has always been a bit suspect defensively, but his criticism doesn't bring me down, it inspires me with the will to do better. He makes me believe that it is in my power to do better. It's very confidence building. Before a game he'll remind us, 'Watch out for them making runs behind your back. You've got to pay attention all the time.' When someone as imposing as Patrick tells you that, it gets you on your toes and ready to go for it as soon as the first whistle blows.

It was Patrick, along with Rémi Garde, who started the flow of French faces into Highbury back in 1996. After them came Manu Petit and Gilles Grimandi in 1997, Thierry Henry in 1999 and Sylvain Wiltord and me in 2000, and there are plenty of other young players in the reserves waiting to make their mark, either at Arsenal or elsewhere. Jérémie Aliadière is a promising forward who scored in a Premiership game at home to West Bromwich Albion in August 2002, while David Grondin went back to France with AS Cannes, and Guy Demel played at Borussia Dortmund after his time at Highbury. As long as there is a French coach here, we French players will have a chance to play for the club, with the fans and the players benefiting from this so-called 'French Connection'. The supporters have adopted us as their own, but we have to thank Patrick for leading the way and making this possible.

I've known him for ten years, since we found ourselves playing alongside each other in the France under-20s squad. It's easy playing with him – he works his socks off in his role as a defensive midfielder, mopping up in front of the back-line, and his game has come on in leaps and bounds over the last few years. He's untouchable now and will surely win the *Ballon d'Or* (the award given by *France Football* magazine for the game's outstanding talents) one day. You can bet his presence will rub off on the Brazilians Edu and Gilberto Silva, his central midfield partners at Highbury. He has been continually linked to Real Madrid, but if Arsenal were ever prepared to sell him they'd leave themselves open to accusations of lacking ambition. He's irreplaceable.

But he's not the only one. There's also Thierry Henry. Titi is a friend and I owe him a lot, not only because he put me up when I first arrived in London, but because he helped me settle in other ways, too: he opened my eyes to London, to Arsenal, and took me on board as his mate. In some ways, his generosity reminds me of my father, Antonio. My dad would save up for months to be able to buy me a pair of boots so that I could play properly; in a sense, Thierry has done the same for me since I came to Arsenal. He's gone out of his way to make me feel welcome.

During the 2002 World Cup he took a lot of flak for

getting himself sent off against Uruguay for one dodgy tackle in our goalless draw. I would point out that the referee's reaction was harsh to say the least, and had Thierry committed the same foul in the Premiership he would not have been punished as severely.

He certainly proved his quality en route to becoming the leading League scorer in England during that successful 2001/02 campaign, and it was his display against Manchester United which turned our season around. Prior to that game we'd been doing very well away from home, but we'd dropped far too many points at Highbury. We were struggling. We'd dominate sides, but would be caught on the break and pegged back. Bolton drew 1–1 in north London; Charlton went one better and beat us 4–2 in a game we dominated from start to finish. We should have been hammering sides like them. But that United game changed things round. We went a goal down but ended up thrashing them 3–1, and Thierry was outstanding. Poor Fabien Barthez in the United goal had an absolute stinker, but that game was the turnaround. Those relative new-comers to the squad like myself, Sylvain Wiltord and the Cameroonian Lauren had been at the club a year by then and knew the English game much better. Of the other new faces, Sol Campbell was used to playing in the Premier League and was desperate for success, while Giovanni van Bronckhorst had been one of the best players in the Scottish league. There was nothing out there to catch us unawares. Together, we just got better and better.

At the turn of the year we really found our rhythm. We'd

lost 3–1 to Newcastle in December, but that was the last time we tasted defeat that season. Liverpool were beaten at Anfield a few days later, despite Giovanni being sent off, and we even thrashed Juventus 3–1 in the Champions League at home. The news that Arsène had signed a new contract at the club clearly helped, but we were unstoppable anyway. We didn't care what United were doing, how strong Leeds looked on paper, or whether Liverpool were lurking at our shoulders; we just swept all before us.

The only time when I wondered whether we might go through a dodgy spell was after our elimination from Europe with a 1–0 loss against Juve in Turin. That cost us a place in the last eight, though we were still unfortunate that Bayer Leverkusen conjured up an unlikely victory over Deportivo La Coruña in Spain to knock us out. Defeat and a rather knee-jerk reaction from the press could have prompted self-doubt, so it was a sign of how strong we were collectively that we responded magnificently by winning a tricky game at Villa Park 2–1.

Lots of people said I scaled new heights with my decisive goal against Villa. It was certainly one of the best I've scored in my career. Freddie Ljungberg sent me away with a long pass upfield and I found myself confronted by George Boateng, only to lift the ball over his head and leave him for dead. That took me one on one with Peter Schmeichel. My first intention was to lob him – not so easy given his size and presence – and although I hesitated momentarily, that's what I ended up doing. I could only have been two metres from the giant Danish keeper, but I still got the angles right to send the ball spiralling into the corner. I've done that before in training, when you're not playing at such pace and can try things for fun, but never in a match.

The Player of the Year award given by UK football writers that I picked up at the end of the season reflected as much on my team-mates as it did on me. You can't succeed in football alone; this is a team game, and thanks to their efforts I was able to make an impact during the 2001/02 season before my knee injury cut short my campaign. My team-mates know my qualities and appreciate what I can bring to the team's play. If I gather possession on the left wing and then decide to run cross-field on to the right flank, the other players don't have a go at me, because they know I might pull something out of the bag and create a chance. But I have to thank my team-mates for allowing me to come out of my shell. I'm aware that it took me time to adapt to Arsenal's style during my first year at the club, as it did to adapt to a new environment and country. But, in time, foreign players can integrate themselves alongside the homegrown stars, and together we can flourish.

I'm proud to have won the Player of the Year award and I'm not convinced by the suggestion that I got it as some sort of consolation prize for not having the chance to play in the 2002 World Cup with France. Most of the votes had been cast long before I suffered my injury, so there's no way I got the sympathy vote. I also think (and I know this sounds corny, but I do believe it) that it was an award for the Arsenal fans. At this club, loyalty knows no bounds and I've never heard us booed. The relationship between the fans and the players in this country is unique. There are no barriers between the stands where the fans sit and the players on the pitch and this closeness makes the atmosphere very intense. If you show a nice piece of skill, you know you'll be applauded, and to hear the roar of the fans behind you is an unbelievable feeling. As you may imagine! That's what inspired me to such a great season last year, and I hope it can do the same in 2002/03 too.

I love it here. For the first time in years I'm playing with freedom in my game and in my life in general. I feel at home at Highbury, and after everything that happened at Marseille, that's so refreshing.

6

Singing *Les Bleus*

I plead guilty. I wasn't on the plane to South Korea for the World Cup, so I wasn't on the pitch when my France team-mates were eliminated at the first stage of the tournament. However, I still feel guilty . . . guilty, like the other players, of taking my mind off the job in the build-up to the competition.

When we should have been focusing on defending our title, we, the champions of 1998, had allowed ourselves to be distracted. Whenever we had a chance we should have been resting aching limbs, conscious of the work we'd have to put in in the Far East, but instead some of the time we had was wasted. We spent days filming a television advertisement, exhausting work, instead of preparing. In hindsight, we should have turned down even the most attractive offers to get ourselves fit and mentally ready for South Korea.

But there was arrogance and complacency too, and I'm as guilty of that as anyone. Before the World Cup I said publicly that I wanted to fly out to the Far East to link up with my team–mates before the semi–final because I was convinced that they would reach that stage of the competition without any difficulty at all. In the end, that was nothing but wishful thinking. June 2002 was a terrible month for me and for France. The fact that the lads were on the other side of the world didn't make the pain or the sorrow of seeing *Les Bleus* eliminated at the first hurdle any easier to take. We'd thrown away the title we'd fought so hard to win four years earlier. There are reasons for the failure. As you'd expect, I've thought about it quite a lot since but it still smarts, an opportunity wasted carelessly and unforgivably.

From the first minute of the World Cup opener against Senegal, it wasn't 'my' France team out there, the side that had waltzed to victory in 1998 and repeated the dose just as spectacularly over in Belgium and Holland two years later. It was painful and weird watching the lads on the telly. They were so off colour and disjointed, I didn't recognise any of them.

In that game against Senegal, all of whose team played their football in France, we put in a dismal performance. I saw a side lacking any sparkle, any zest, a pale shadow of the team that had swept all before them at the World Cup four years earlier and at Euro 2000. From the start it was obvious that the players were knackered. When you're playing in a tournament of that size and you're not tuned in mentally or physically, anyone can beat you. Unfortunately, that's exactly what happened to us. France 0 Senegal 1 would have been considered a shock result before the game, but watching the match itself we were lucky to get nil.

As soon as we'd lost that match, I knew it would take a Herculean effort to get back on track and go on to retain our title. The writing was effectively on the wall because in a tournament that is that tight it's virtually impossible to pick yourselves up after starting with such a demoralising defeat. Some teams have managed it in the past, notably Argentina in 1990 when they lost their opening match to Cameroon but still made the final, but you're in a downward spiral and your opponents know you can be beaten. As players you are aware of that as well, and the fact that you are conscious that you're not quite ready physically just plays on your mind.

Nevertheless, I spoke publicly after the Senegal game and stressed that hope still remained, that all was not lost and this France team was still hungry for success. I was hoping to gee the lads up, but I still stand by those comments. The main problem didn't boil down to the standard of the opposition or a lack of motivation among *Les Bleus*, but simply to tiredness. The two subsequent group games against Uruguay (0–0) and Denmark (0–2) merely showed that this exhausted team, however good it was on paper, was incapable of mustering up even a single goal. There might have been a bit of bad luck on the way, particularly for David Trézéguet with his uncanny ability to hit post or bar, and we might have fallen foul of Uruguay's spoiling tactics (what was that about, given that we were down to ten men?), but at no time during the tournament did the France team show their true colours. We caved in and lost everything.

Before the tournament had begun, I'd warned people not to underestimate Brazil. They'd been written off mainly as a result of their disappointing qualifying campaign, during which they'd lost six times – the most defeats they'd ever suffered en route to the finals. Silvinho, my former Arsenal team-mate and a typical Brazilian-type full-back with attack on the brain, told me that Brazil's reputation goes before them in the South American qualifiers and makes getting to the World Cup even harder than the finals themselves. He was proved right.

Brazil deserved to win the title. For all Germany's achievement in reaching the final, with Oliver Kahn a goalkeeper at the very top of his game and Michael Ballack using the biggest stage on which to show off his class, I was delighted to see Felipe Scolari's side do so well. The sight of Ronaldo putting his nightmare at France 98 and all those years lost to a knee injury behind him was wonderful, and encouraged me to think I might do the same once I'd recovered.

Without blowing my own trumpet too much, I also suggested before the World Cup that we should keep an eye on Senegal. Their players learned their trade in the French league and have proved their quality now. Look how many have come to England since the tournament. El Hadji Diouf and Salif Diao will be excellent signings for Liverpool, while Aliou Cissé's leadership could help Birmingham retain their place in the top flight. My own skills as a pundit probably end there, however, particularly as I thought France would play England in the quarter-finals. But, in truth, as far as I was concerned this wasn't about Brazil, Senegal or England. People at home in France were only asking me one question: 'What went wrong for *Les Bleus*?'

Suffice to say our past caught up with us badly in South Korea. By 'past' I mean the exhausting season the French internationals had been through, because virtually all of us had just finished a busy, jam-packed campaign at club level. We'd also gone to Australia and Chile with *Les Bleus*; personally, I took three weeks to get over that trip to Santiago, and a few of my colleagues experienced similar problems. All that travelling beggared belief and really took its toll; hopefully the FFF have learned their lesson now. All that fatigue which built up in the months leading up to the tournament was at the heart of why France fared so badly in the Far East.

People have come back at me by saying that it wasn't just the French players who had experienced long seasons. Surely it was the same for all the other countries as well? I'd argue that's not the case. Virtually every player in the French squad played at the very best clubs across Europe and therefore my team-mates were competing at the top of their domestic leagues or in the latter stages of the Champions League, playing on average a relentless three games a week en route. Of the 23 who did go to South Korea, only the likes of Youri Djorkaeff, who had joined Bolton and helped them stay in the Premiership, and Frank

Leboeuf at Marseille were not involved near the top of their domestic leagues at the end of the season. If I hadn't been injured in the build-up to the tournament, no doubt I would have experienced the same problems as my team-mates over there. I wouldn't have been in any better condition than any of the other lads. As it was, my knee injury had been punishment enough for playing too much. Injury may be an everyday hazard for a sportsman, but so too is fatigue.

When you're at the top everyone loves you. After a defeat, no one wants to know you. That's when you start asking yourself questions and can become hyper self-critical. In all honesty, you need the odd setback to help you progress in the long-term. Too many victories, too many compliments and you start thinking it's all too easy. You let your guard down and eventually slip up. It's easy to get carried away with your own publicity when you're playing at the highest level. Now, though, the opposite is the case. With *Les Bleus'* title lost, the knee-jerk reaction in France has virtually propelled us back to square one with everything we achieved virtually forgotten, the memories wiped by the failure in South Korea. You can't forget what we won, but it feels as if some of the critics have.

From the comfort of my armchair, I suffered watching Marcel Desailly and the lads stumbling from one disaster to another at the finals – no wins, no goals, elimination with barely a whimper. I was working as an expert analyser for TF1, the French television station, and I was interviewed about all the France games for some kind of technical overview of the team's displays. Some people have asked me whether I was privately relieved not to be involved in such a depressing campaign, but that never crossed my mind. I would have given anything to be with the French team in the Far East, even as our dreams sank without trace. I felt involved, and it felt wrong to be so far away while my friends and team-mates were suffering. It really got to me watching it all on the telly.

I got the impression that people thought I'd not been adequately replaced in the squad. Sure, a left-winger willing to track back provides a vital link between defence and attack, but contrary to what was said and written at the time, I think the forwards like Sylvain Wiltord who played in my place did a decent job. They just lacked some luck. In all three games, they hit the goalkeeper's legs or the woodwork; if those shots had gone in, it would have painted a totally different picture.

The other factor to take into account was our status as pre-tournament favourites. In 1998, the French team had been considered outsiders, at best, as challengers for the title because we were playing at home. As a result, it was easier for us to catch our opponents unawares. In Korea, France were the big favourites and everyone's tip to become the first European side to win the title outside their home continent. There was no surprise element involved at all. The three teams we came up against were naturally cautious and set their stall out – they were the surprise elements, not us. Uruguay were so cagey we could still be playing now and they wouldn't yet have considered venturing over the halfway line. Senegal, too, sat back and hit us on the break.

I would have liked the opportunity to see if I could have made a difference but, that said, I'm happy to have picked up the injury when I did rather than during the World Cup itself. I told that to a journalist from the French newspaper *Le Figaro* back in Paris in May 2002. I was still on crutches then, but all hell broke out as a result. People accused me of being unpatriotic, of putting petty club football ahead of the national team, but if I'd gone to Korea and ruptured my knee ligaments over there I wouldn't have been available for Arsenal until the beginning of 2003 at the very earliest, and it's my club who pays my wages. I took plenty of flak, but I don't take any of those words back. Bonuses apart, French Football Federation doesn't pay my way. I have a duty to my club, as any employee has to his employer. After all, it's my performances at club level that give me the opportunity to represent my country.

People ask sometimes if you can choose between your club and your country, if you can prioritise. I just say it's impossible to choose between the two. When an argument broke out between Arsenal and the French team officials over the state of my knee during the spring before the World Cup, I found myself caught in the crossfire. The doctors from the two camps were not the same so, predictably enough, they came up with different plans of action. Arsenal ruled out my participation in the finals almost immediately and were keen for me to have surgery straight away to get me ready for the next domestic season; the national team doctors advised me to wait, hoping that the knee might heal naturally and I might even be back on my feet in time for the tournament. Common sense told me I wouldn't be on the plane to Asia, even if I was praying for a miracle, but in that period of doubt I didn't want to let my feelings be known publicly. Why? Because I didn't want to have to choose one or the other. My loyalties were divided.

On the one hand, to represent the national team is so important. I know that. But on the other hand, I'm aware that to be picked for the France side I need to be playing regularly in a championship like the Premiership. You can only play international football if you're doing well at club level. My employer was Arsenal, and they were the ones who paid my salary each week. I couldn't forget that. When you play for France you earn only match fees or win bonuses. The money is important, but it's sporadic and it's not enough from which to earn a living.

I'm sure Aimé Jacquet, who'd coached us to the World Cup in 1998, would have responded in exactly the same way as the then coach Roger Lemerre did. Roger had the same ideas as Aimé on the importance of club football. He spoke to us in his own way; he was Aimé's right-hand man during the World Cup in 1998 and didn't change his frank, direct methods once he'd assumed the reins himself. Thierry Henry, Patrick Vieira and Sylvain Wiltord were his 'little Gunners'. He loves English football. Whenever he welcomed us to training camp, he would ask, 'And how are my little Gunners, then?' The crucial word being 'my'. We belonged to him and he protected us. That's the link between national and club football.

Playing for your club or your country generates different emotions. At Metz I'd learned how to be a good professional playing in the Premier Division, but being selected for the France team introduced me to football at the highest level. The games are different as well: at club level your team-mates are driven on by their determination to succeed, but at international level your team-mates are playing with pure passion and it's instinctive. With your club you can take three touches of the ball before passing it on, whereas you have to collect and give immediately at the higher level because everything happens ten times quicker.

Yet the two levels do have similarities. In both cases, I find myself effectively acting as a standard bearer. When you play for a foreign club you have to create the best possible image of a French footballer. The Premiership is one of the most respected and watched leagues in the world and the French players, not only at Arsenal but at Manchester United and Chelsea, were forever conscious of upholding the country's status as world champions. Even though we've lost that crown, you still have to live up to that reputation; all the French players in England, whether they are internationals or not, are ambassadors for their country. I like 'representing my country' at club level.

Of course, the ambition of every French footballer is to wear that trademark blue shirt. At the end of every international game the tradition is to swap shirts with your opponents, but I'm always reluctant to give mine up. I prefer to take my blue one home rather than anyone else's.

When you're young you're desperate to take part in

every competition you can, international tournaments obviously attracting you most of all. The announcement of an international squad, putting on the blue shirt, hearing the *Marseillaise* being played over the loudspeakers – you remember even the smallest details. Experiencing every little part of what every French player aspires to really conjures up marvellous emotions.

I had never been called up by the junior or French youth team selectors, so to be finally picked for the national under-20s made me feel ten feet tall. I was selected for the squad and made my first appearance in a 2–1 win over Denmark on 7 December 1993. Since that victory I've never known anything but good times wearing the tricolour on my chest. Mine was a talented generation, and I find myself playing at Arsenal with two of my team-mates from back then in Patrick Vieira and Sylvain Wiltord.

One of my closest friends as I progressed from the under-20s was Florian Maurice. Flo played at Olympique Lyonnais, I was at Metz, but we played together with the French team. With the under-20s we managed to qualify for the Olympic Games in Atlanta in 1996. Before we left for the United States I met François Brisson, another former Lyon striker who had won the Olympic tournament with the French team back in 1984 in Los Angeles. That was the first time professionals had been admitted into the Games. I flicked through some old photos of their victory with François and cracked up at the sight of their three-coloured tracksuits which seemed so out of date. We didn't do as well in Atlanta as Brisson had in 1984, but that Olympic tournament was still my first real taste of representing my country on a big stage.

Experiencing the Olympic Games is incredible for any young footballer. The idea that only professionals under 20 years of age can take part is great. The Games retain a unique flavour, though any international competition designed for youngsters helps you develop as a player: it's all part of your apprenticeship, and at 15, 16, 17 or 18 years old you become aware, little by little, of what it means to represent your country. You learn from the French Football Federation's coaches as well as from your team-mates who have come from other clubs. Together, you take on other nations, whether big or small, who are intent on beating France because of our reputation and past successes. You learn to struggle; you learn to win. We might have come back from Atlanta without a medal but we had all grown up a little bit. After that, everything fell into place.

Out of all the countries I've been picked to play against, one in particular is dear to me: Portugal. Down there, near Oporto where my father was born, I feel as if they would have loved it if I'd gone on to play in their colours. But even if Pires sounds like a Portuguese name, I was born in France; it was in France that I set about becoming a footballer, and it was France who offered me my first taste of international football. Wearing the blue shirt, I had no qualms about crossing swords with my Portuguese cousins out on the pitch. In fact, I would go on to play against them in one of my first matches for the full France team, a friendly in Braga, only a few kilometres from where I used to go on holiday as a child with my parents.

In Atlanta we had a closely knit squad, but Patrick Vieira was injured and had to go home early. Even so, we progressed as far as the quarter-finals where, despite an equaliser from Florian, we were eliminated 2–1 by a golden goal . . . by Portugal, no less. That was a setback I later avenged at Euro 2000 where I helped knock out my father's compatriots 2–1 in the semi-final, also with a golden goal. In fact, Portugal is also going to be where I may next taste a big international tournament, as they will host Euro 2004. I'd love to make up for missing the World Cup there.

The Portuguese often seem to stand in the way of *Les Bleus* at major competitions. I remember that legendary semi-final at Euro 84 we won 3–2 with Michel Platini & Co. lighting up Marseille with their skill and exuberance. That game had everything – suspense, intensity and, ultimately, victory. But that's not always the way with us against the Portuguese. I met Eric Cantona in Manchester towards the end of the 2000/01 season after we'd just beaten Tottenham 2–1 at Old Trafford in the FA Cup semi-final. He'd attended the match, and as we chatted in the dressing rooms afterwards I told him I'd seen him playing in the beach soccer World Cup on the telly. His France side had been knocked out by Portugal . . .

Out of the crop of under-20s, Florian Maurice and I were two of the first to make the step up to the full French side. A different world awaited us. Euro 96 had just taken place in England. An ageing France side had been knocked out in the semi-finals on penalties by the Czech Republic, and at the end of the summer Aimé Jacquet wanted to inject a bit of young blood into his squad. Flo and I were picked and we arrived rather tentatively at our first training session with the full side.

When you arrive at Clairefontaine, the FFF's technical centre just south-west of Paris, you immediately feel a bit intimidated. You go through past the warden at the entrance and find yourself on a narrow pathway leading up to the chateau. I'd played on the pitches around the complex while training with the under-20s, but I'd only ever seen the castle from a distance. That was where the senior team stayed, not the juniors, and we'd look up at it and mutter to ourselves, 'Shit, when am I going to get a chance to stay up there?' When that chance comes you initially feel completely lost, what with all the rooms, corridors and outhouses. You haven't got a clue where you're going. Of course you get used to them quickly enough, and nowadays I never want to leave.

During that first call-up in September 1996 I was as overawed when we ate our meals as when we were out on the training pitch. I felt like a little kid surrounded by his idols – Didier Deschamps, Marcel Desailly, Laurent Blanc . . . Next to these established, recognised internationals, I was virtually a mesmerised fan all over again. I'd already represented my country at junior and under-20s levels, but in this team I was so overawed by the players around me wearing the blue shirt with the golden cock on the breast that I shrank back into my shell and couldn't play. When you're only 22 or 23 and you suddenly find yourself in the

France side, you know full well that you're taking a huge step and you can't slip up. The authority and experience of Dédé, Marcel and Lolo struck me from the off. I just lost concentration among all these big-name stars. My own game disintegrated. I felt like a little kid, wet behind the ears. Still, the captain Dédé Deschamps made a point of introducing himself to me and wished me the best of luck. 'I hope you go as far in the game as you can,' he said. When you've just arrived at Clairefontaine for the first time, being told something like that really hits home. Hopefully, one day, I'll be able to say the same thing to young players arriving for their first game. One day.

We were preparing, me and my new team-mates, or should I say idols, for a friendly against Mexico on 31 August but I found all the training drills really tough. Technically, compared to my club, this was in a different league. I was surrounded by the very best French players and the difference was striking. All the drills were executed at a quicker speed compared to club level, with moves and passes made instinctively. I'd never seen dribbling like it.

I'll never forget the match itself. I made my debut as a half-time substitute that night at Parc des Princes, replacing Reynald Pedros (then at Nantes). As is the tradition with the France team, as the debutant I kept the match pennant as a souvenir. We won 2–0, and it opened my eyes to football at the top level. I watched and I learned.

At first, every match I played for *Les Bleus* seemed hard. I was only a pale shadow of my real self. I was called up quite regularly, but mentally I wasn't ready yet. In fact, I was almost paralysed so desperate was I to do well. When I started a game I wouldn't be any good because, even for friendlies, the occasion just left me too tense. All I could think about was that I was representing France, and that would just go through my head over and over again. Furthermore, I considered myself a small, inexperienced player who was playing with the big boys. Metz was a small club compared to some of the other teams in France, small fry in terms of their finances and their 'stars', but while that spurred us on to try to turn the big boys over, when I found myself alongside the best players in the country I just foundered. I was reduced to a timid little player, overawed by the occasion, but I was happy. During the games and training sessions I'd learn plenty, and it was my ability to pick things up that eventually allowed me to express myself properly. At this level, every little titbit of information is a lesson to be learned.

Among the landmarks that punctuate an international career, your first goal is something you never forget. Mine wasn't a significant goal for the team, but it still stands out during my time with *Les Bleus* as a symbol of my development, opening up a new road along which I'm still travelling. I scored it on my second cap, a friendly against Turkey on 9 October 1996 at Parc des Princes. We won 4–0 that night and I got off the mark with a lobbed goal. I often remember my goals as having been 'nice' to score, but that one simply opened my international account and confirmed our victory. After all, what's the point of scoring a good goal unless the team wins? I don't look back on my goals as individual incidents; what's important is that they help bring victory, warming the hearts of both my team-mates and our supporters.

Having said that, that goal lobbed beyond the Turkish goalkeeper did take a weight off my mind. Subconsciously, to score, especially if it contributes to a win, frees up a player and shows you've put in a performance. It's not as if you've made it, but it's remembered by the public, the other players and, of course, the statisticians, and that helps. Setting up goals has always given me more pleasure than scoring them myself, but that goal against Turkey was my first for my country and confirmed that I was justifying my selection for the full squad.

The French team later left Parc des Princes to take up its new home in the Stade de France. During the spring of 1997 I went along with Didier Deschamps and Zinédine Zidane to the building site that was steadily becoming our main arena for the 1998 World Cup. The stadium was already magnificent, but amid the cranes, the diggers and the mud it was hard to imagine this would be the pitch on which we'd win the tournament. I remember the first game in that ground, against Spain in January 1998. During that match I felt still more at ease; I didn't start the game, but running out on to that frozen pitch after 62 minutes to replace Ibrahim Ba was another major step up for me in my development with the team. We won 1–0 thanks to a goal scored by Zidane.

The France team is assembled only in the build-up to

competitive or friendly games, so it doesn't have the continuity of a club side. Players drop out and others replace them to make up the squad, but together we are a type of family. Between the players and the management staff there's a real closeness, and at the heart of this set-up I've discovered some really endearing personalities, like Emmanuel Petit whom I'd never played with or against at club level. In France, when I moved south to play for Marseille, he had already left Monaco to join Arsenal; in England, when I joined Arsenal he'd just transferred to Barcelona. Life in Spain didn't really work out for Manu; like me, his career flourished on this side of the Channel. We are both in London at the moment with him playing at Chelsea, but we only really got to know each other through our time in the full France squad. I like his attitude to things. He gets his priorities right.

The Premiership also showed the strength of character of people like Christian Karembeu. Although he'd been shamefully booed while playing for France – for example, during our 5–0 win over Japan in the spring of 2001 – he demonstrated his experience week after week with his former club Middlesbrough. He scored four League goals that season, exactly the same number as me, but the crucial difference is that his enabled Boro to retain their place in the top flight. Christian sees his role as a footballer as that of an actor performing in a play; that's also my vision.

The personalities of the France team players are all interesting. Nicolas Anelka, now at Manchester City but previously with Arsenal and Liverpool, is another significant one. He was another of the 'Frenchies' who advised me to accept the challenge at Highbury. Nico has been in and out of late and was overlooked for the World Cup, but he deserves to be in the national team because of his quality and work-rate on the pitch.

But the one who amazes me most of all is, of course, Zinedine Zidane. Football is at the core of his being. Everyone knows about his qualities, and no one comes close to him, even in training, with his dribbles, his feints, his swerves, his flicks. It would be impossible to list all his moves and it would be impossible to imitate them. Then again, just by trying to be half as good as him you improve your own game. His absence through injury during the first two games in South Korea undoubtedly cost us dear. Roger Lemerre's favoured 4–2–3–1 formation cried out for Zizou sitting behind David Trézéguet in an attacking midfield role, and neither Youri Djorkaeff, Christophe Dugarry or Johan Micoud managed to fill the void his absence left. When Zinedine did come back against Denmark, the game was already up. Zizou is the master, our artistic inspiration. We really missed him.

Much was made in the build-up to the 2002 World Cup of the culture of victory that had previously flourished in the French system. The drip-down of experience from the various generations that make up the team helped make that possible. The likes of Deschamps, Desailly and Blanc understood the need to share experiences and hand them down to the next crop of youngsters. Laurent Blanc will always be a natural leader. Didier Deschamps has been a real inspiration supporting his team-mates; Marcel Desailly, with his discreet style, will do likewise in that role from now on. We found ourselves talking about our backgrounds one evening during Euro 2000. Marcel was telling us about his upbringing in Ghana, and there was me with my childhood in Champagne. Talking about football is important, but talking about life is better.

Back in the spring of 1998, I was playing for Metz and we were about to be pipped at the last in the race for the French title, but with the national team everything was up in the air. Was I going to take part in the World Cup? Would Aimé Jacquet want me in the squad? A few weeks before the tournament, in May, I was at home in Metz having a siesta when the telephone rang. My wife had just heard the list of the 28 players selected for the initial squad for the World Cup on the radio. 'Robby, you're in!' she screamed. She was ecstatic and I was in a state of shock. It didn't click with me at first. It was only a few days later when I was talking with my friends who have nothing to do with football that it really sank in that I was going to the World Cup. I was going to be representing France, participating in the competition about which every footballer dreams.

I linked up with the rest of the 28-man party at Clairefontaine conscious that six of us would not be in the final squad which was to be announced a few days later. Aimé Jacquet had named six extra players just in case any of us suffered an injury or a sudden loss of form at the last minute. But that larger squad soon settled down and worked well together, and I felt fairly relaxed about it all.

The younger players, like me, weren't aware that our international futures were on the line.

At the end of May we had to endure a very difficult evening. I remember it well. I was on the ground floor of the main building, next to a table-tennis table, when six of my team-mates strode past dressed in civvies. I asked them what they were doing. 'The coach called us together and saw us one by one in his office . . .' Almost in tears, they told the rest of us that they were not going to be taking part in the tournament. They were trying to order taxis to take them back to Paris. We watched our friends packing their bags and leaving. Nicolas Anelka, Ibrahim Ba, Martin Djetou, Pierre Laigle, Lionel Letizi and Sabri Lamouchi disappeared that night. It was as if Clairefontaine had been gripped by a cold snap; I felt sorry for them all. Apart from Anelka, I knew Lionel Letizi best because I played alongside him at Metz. I was also close to Martin Djetou. I found it too hard to go and speak to them. What can you say to one of your team-mates who has not been picked when you have? They had half an hour to pack their bags and that was it, their dream was over. After they had left I sat and contemplated my future: I would be playing in the World Cup in the year that France was the host.

As it was, I spent more of that World Cup on the bench than out on the pitch, but our group was so tight that it hardly seemed to matter who was selected and who had to sit it out. After our first-round matches and a relatively comfortable qualification, we faced Paraguay in the second round. I retained my place in the 16-man squad for the game, but I didn't start the match. We knew less about our opponents than about the European teams, but we knew they possessed talented footballers, in particular their goalkeeper Luis José Chilavert who went on to play for Strasbourg in the French championship. He proved his quality in the 90 minutes, saving everything we threw at him, and almost single-handedly took the game to extra-time. For the first time in the World Cup, our qualification depended on penalties or a golden goal.

When you're a substitute you pay as much attention to the game as you would normally, but you're not as apprehensive or as nervous as if you were out there in the starting line-up. Your preparation is different if you know you're on the bench and you approach the game in a far more relaxed way. There isn't as much pressure on you from the off, and psychologically you're more detached from the action. But at the same time you have to be careful not to cut yourself off from the team. The worst thing that can happen is if you allow yourself to become a spectator. Retaining your concentration, your impulse, is essential if you're going to react well when called upon. You have to be ready when the coach asks you to warm up, which is what happened when Aimé Jacquet called me over before introducing me into the action at the Felix Bollaert stadium in Lens.

Thankfully, I was alert enough to play my part and set up the golden goal for Laurent Blanc. My involvement in that goal gave me a wonderful sense of satisfaction, proud as I was to have had a hand in keeping our dream alive. You fret about trying to make your mark, but I did that in Lens. Our victory over the Paraguayans was followed by similarly tense wins over Italy (0–0, 4–3 on penalties) in the quarter-finals and Croatia (2–1) in the semis. Then came our final against Brazil.

France versus Brazil. It was the final the whole country had hoped for and a chance for *Les Bleus* to lock horns with the famous yellow shirts, which conjured up memories of great figures from the past, like Pelé. For me, the match had a particular significance because I could hear Portuguese, the language my father had taught me, echoing round the corridors of the Stade de France. My Portuguese is not perfect so I didn't catch everything that was said, but I took in some of the words. When you're out on the pitch you talk with your team-mates, but it's always useful to be able to understand what your opponents are chatting about as well.

I used to dream of coming up against Brazil. Before the World Cup I'd actually predicted a France versus Brazil final. It wasn't a premonition, just what I really wanted to happen. Could you imagine a better match? I'd been a member of the squad, if not in the starting line-up, at Le Tournoi in 1997 when we'd played Brazil in Lyon. I'd been thrown on to the pitch to join a French side that included Flo Maurice and Marc Keller, who went on to score our goal to ensure the match ended 1–1. Later, when selected for the Confederations Cup in June 2001, I scored one of our two goals in a 2–1 semi-final win over Brazil before our victory in the final against Japan (1–0). However, out of all these games against the Brazilians, and even though I didn't play an active role, the best one was still the final in 1998. The way we won that match was so straightforward, the sequence of events in the final so perfect. It was a dream game.

Everyone in France followed *Les Bleus'* World Cup campaign. Everything, from the games to behind the scenes, was filmed, but certain moments escaped the microphones and the cameras. During a competition, some privacy is necessary to allow the group to bond away from the cameras. It's only in hindsight that we can recognise certain key moments, such as the stuff which went on in the changing rooms before the final.

As we were getting ready we heard people outside the dressing room asking each other, 'Is Ronaldo going to play or what?' Clearly, something was up. The backroom staff kept us informed of each new rumour, telling us, 'Look, he's going to play. Oh, hold on. No, he's not. He's not well and he's not playing . . .' Frankly, it didn't matter whether he was going to take part or not. Ronaldo was not our problem. Every one of us – those lucky enough to be selected out on the pitch, those of us named as substitutes, as well as those of us left out altogether – knew exactly what we had to do. We had to concentrate on our jobs. We had only one thing in mind: to prove that this France team was capable of winning the World Cup. Beating Brazil, with or without Ronaldo, would achieve that objective.

Even now I hear people saying we won only because Ronaldo wasn't on form that day. That's not true. That evening, France were stronger in every part of the pitch. No one can really say otherwise, regardless of Ronaldo's epileptic fit and all the questions that threw up. We hammered Brazil.

Apart from all the agitation in the changing rooms about whether Ronaldo was in or out, our preparation for the match had been perfect. Aimé Jacquet outlined his tactics, stressing how important our set-pieces would be and reminding us how vulnerable Brazil were in defence. Aimé had watched many videos of Brazil and his analysis was spot on. Zizou twice headed in corners, and when Manu Petit added a third to make it 3–0, the result was a fitting finale for the retiring, but cruelly suspended Blanc, one of the figures who had been the first to inspire our winning mentality. The youngsters in the squad, like me, had just joined in this spiral of success, but we'd soon become a major part of it.

When we climbed the steps on to the podium to collect the cup we were all on cloud nine, carried by the noise from the crowd but also a long way away from them. I felt somehow cut off from the world. What we had just achieved seemed so enormous. Receiving the trophy was magical. We were lined up, all impatient to get our hands on the cup. When Dédé Deschamps lifted it I had flashbacks to Maradona, Pelé and all those legendary footballers doing the same. I knew that a few seconds after my captain I would get a chance to do the same.

I found myself standing between Zinedine Zidane and Marcel Desailly, who would go on to become the French captain. I climbed up in turn on to the platform and looked at the players below me. I had to smile. We didn't have any idea of what our victory would do for the country, but we still knew we'd achieved something remarkable. I can't remember which one of my team-mates handed me the trophy, but when you have the cup in your hands you instinctively raise it to your lips and kiss it. I was holding the World Cup! I wanted to be selfish and run away with it, but realised that I'd get rugby tackled to the ground so I thought better of it and handed it on, still pinching myself, to the next man.

After the World Cup, Aimé Jacquet retired as national coach to take up a role as technical director at the FFF and Roger Lemerre took up the reins. Our victory in 1998 was testament to the qualities of the group of players we had, but also to the preparations we had been put through on the training pitch.

At club level, because we play so much, training is more about maintaining fitness levels and basic skills. At international level sessions are completely different, aimed at getting us ready for a tournament like the World Cup that can last for up to a month. To get into the rhythm we need to adopt to do our best in the tournament, the coaches take a three-pronged attack to training with physical, technical and tactical work. The squad is divided into groups, one for the defenders, one for the attackers. Defensive midfielders join the latter group, attacking midfielders the former.

The most important work we do centres on our tactical

approach. We learn how to move as a unit, whether it be the defensive line, the midfield or the forwards progressing up or retreating back down the pitch. Practising these moves over and over again makes it second nature when we come to play a match. In international football you don't have the time to look up and search for one of your team-mates, you have to know instinctively where he is.

Roger Lemerre would repeat, 'Each player is a professional.' It is taken as read that every one of his squad knows what he's doing and we are left free to work on the basics: those of us who want to work on our pace can do so, while anyone wanting to practise shooting, dribbling or ball juggling can do that on his own. We are always aware that the technical staff are ready and willing to help. There are loads of them, but each fills a specific role: René Girard and Guy Stephan were Lemerre's assistant coaches, Bruno Martini took the goalkeepers, while Henri Emile looked after the logistics side. But having them around all the time helped us mentally as well: the knowledge that you are surrounded by such quality backroom staff can often give you the edge in an international and ultimately be the difference between victory and defeat out on the pitch.

I didn't see much difference between the way Aimé Jacquet and Roger Lemerre prepared or trained for a game. In fact, Roger merely maintained the good habits Aimé had implemented during his time in charge of the team. And if any proof was needed that he was as good a coach as his predecessors, it came with our success at Euro 2000.

After the failure at the World Cup in 2002, Roger

Lemerre was replaced by Jacques Santini, the former Saint-Etienne player who had just helped Olympique Lyonnais claim their first ever league title, and someone I hardly knew. We, as players, were not consulted by the FFF over who the new coach should be. In my opinion, the federation should have listened to us, even if they rejected our ideas once they'd heard us. After all, we were the people who would be most affected by the appointment. I felt for Roger. When we were crowned champions of Europe under his leadership, no one paid tribute to his tactical genius. Then, after Korea, he was simply thrown to the dogs. No one deserves that.

I would have liked to see Didier Deschamps appointed as national coach in Roger's stead, but he still has plenty to learn as a manager at Monaco where he's been in charge for only a couple of seasons. Instead, we got Santini who quickly appointed his own backroom staff and settled into the post. In truth, I liked what he said when he announced his first squad to play in the friendly against Tunisia in August 2002. 'I hope Pires will be back with us as soon as possible,' he stressed, which was nice to hear. He also asked me to link up with the squad for that game. While I found his offer kind and reassuring, I declined because I couldn't face being with *Les Bleus* without being able to join in at training or in the match itself. It was too hard.

In any case, it's not as if the France team suddenly needs a miracle to be successful in the future. That game with Tunisia might have ended in a disappointing 1–1 draw, but we still boast the quality to succeed and the world will see as much at Euro 2004, the qualification games for which are already underway. Out on the pitch, Desailly is still the boss and I hope he will continue to lead the side for a long time to come. I heard talk that I was among the pretenders to succeed him as skipper when he finally retires, but I've never put my name forward. That said, if I was ever offered the armband I would certainly consider accepting the honour. Captaining my country would be a proud moment, but when Marcel quits the post there may be better candidates than me to offer the communication and inspirational skills needed for the job. We'll have to see.

Some people might have blocked the memories out after the disaster in Korea, but Roger Lemerre's reign was initially really successful. After our triumph at France 98 we still had to qualify for the European Championship in Holland and Belgium and we were all well aware that no European team had failed to reach the finals having won the World Cup. That presented us with a challenge. Every match was going to be tougher now because, having reached the top, we had to justify our position and maintain it.

I had my own challenge ahead. I had to shed the tag of being a perennial substitute and establish myself as a first-team regular in the national side, and in that respect the qualifying game in Russia in the autumn of 1998 proved pivotal. The game was played in Moscow in horrible conditions on a quagmire of a pitch, but we had to win to stay on course for the finals. To that end, I scored from Nicolas Anelka's cross after 29 minutes and set up the second goal. Fantastic. We all went home happy that night but, while I'd played well and was clearly recognised as a decent player, I still felt that I hadn't established myself as a key player in the team, someone France could not do without. Sure, I'd scored a goal and played a part in another, but I hadn't imposed myself on the game as much as I'd have liked. I was still too cautious, but at least in Moscow I didn't hide during the game; I wanted the ball and was desperate to be involved. I might not have arrived, but I was definitely on the way.

And so to Euro 2000. Being a part of the France 98 winning squad didn't guarantee me a place in Roger Lemerre's set-up – not that I could worry too much about that. My season at Marseille had been so disappointing that I was too busy helping to try to save their Premier Division status to worry about making the France squad, though with our mission accomplished at the Stade Vélodrome it was with some relief that I heard from the coach that I would be involved.

The tournament began well. We had the same motivation and spirit as we'd had on home soil a couple of years earlier, and our status as favourites did not appear to choke us too much out on the pitch. For my part, I was used more by Roger Lemerre than I had been by Aimé, and I could feel the confidence inside me growing with each appearance.

As you will remember, we reached the final where we met the Italians. I'll always compare this match to our game with Paraguay in Lens in 1998: it was a dour, tight, tactical struggle that would eventually be decided by a golden goal. It took Sylvain Wiltord's last-minute equaliser to take the game into extra-time, but from then on in we felt strong, confident, almost unbeatable.

Stuck out on the left wing, I hadn't really made as much impact on the 90 minutes as I'd have liked. Just before the start of the first period of extra-time, Marcel Desailly strode over to me and asked, 'What position are you playing in, exactly?' I didn't really know what to say, but he was right to have a go. He saw my reaction and, job done, added, 'Right then, let's see what you're capable of.'

It did the trick. I remember gathering a pass, bursting forward down the flank, dribbling past an opponent and crossing. It all happened in a flash, but that little flurry of skill was enough to establish me once and for all among the best in the France team. With David Trézéguet reacting in the middle to smash in the golden goal from my cross, setting up that winner was the clincher for my career. Of course, as the ball cannoned into the back of the net and the stadium exploded, I didn't realise the consequences setting up that goal would have for me. I had too many things chasing through my head; everything was blurred. But the most important thing for me at the time was the knowledge that France had won the game; we had beaten Italy and added the European crown to our world title. That was all that mattered.

After receiving the trophy we all gathered on the pitch for an impromptu party. I was there among friends. I danced around with Thierry Henry, Patrick Vieira and

Sylvain Wiltord, soon to become my team-mates at Arsenal, but this team had also become a kind of family for us all too. It wasn't a closed family, we were always welcoming new arrivals and debutants into the team, but the unity and tightness of the group had developed since 1998. Every time I've been back to Clairefontaine since that World Cup success has been a pleasure, and the enjoyment we feel whenever we meet up helps us take every game seriously, whether it be a friendly or a competitive match. When we suffered disappointments – like losing 2–1 to Spain in March 2001, or 2–1 to Chile in September 2001 – we knew how to react because we had confidence in ourselves and, more importantly, in each other.

To that end, the dining room in the castle at Clairefontaine became a key room. We would all sit there together round the table at meal-times. It was as if we were in the Stock Exchange, what with the constant chatter, or should I say shouting, among ourselves.

We were confident in each other's company, and in eachother's ability. But maybe we did lack a certain humility in the build-up to the 2002 World Cup. For example, look at the Adidas advertisement we shot before a ball had been kicked in anger at the tournament. That is why I say I plead guilty. That advert featured us all wearing our trademark blue shirts with two stars above the badge, symbolising the two World Cup wins France was supposed to be celebrating: our triumph in 1998 and, by implication, the win we were supposed to be on the verge of enjoying in Korea and Japan. We were basically saying we'd as good as retained the World Cup already. It might have been a decent advert, but it made me ill at ease.

Even so, the label of *Les Bleus* remains a big seller on the high street, and will do for a long time to come. French players are always trying their hand abroad and tend to make the most successful imports for leagues like Serie A and the Premiership. But the French brand is also marketed by our coaches – Arsène Wenger and Gérard Houllier in England, Bruno Metsu formerly with Senegal and Philippe Troussier in Japan, and others besides. They're the best in the world. Maybe it's down to the outstanding grounding they received in France as well as the desire and passion, a bit of magic that you can't teach, they all share. Their ability to communicate that to their sides marks them out as special.

Now that Jacques Santini has taken over as manager, I hope he gives youth a chance at the top level. He appears to be doing that already. Philippe Mexès, Anthony Réveillère and Sidney Govou were in his first squad, and Liverpool's Bruno Cheyrou replaced the injured Thierry Henry for the first qualifier against Cyprus – and these youngsters are really talented. For us older players, it will be a challenge to keep our places in the team, but new blood is always beneficial.

In the build-up to the World Cup in 2002, the core of the France team remained essentially the same though new players did make their mark as well, players you knew well from having come across them at club level. There were youngsters like Jérémie Bréchet (Lyon) and Mikaël Silvestre

(Manchester United), established players from the French top flight like Eric Carrière (previously with Nantes and now at Lyon), and others who left France to play in England like Laurent Robert (formerly with PSG and now working wonders with Newcastle) or Steve Marlet (Lyon to Fulham). These guys came into the reckoning for our 2001 Confederations Cup campaign when we were without Zidane and Henry, and they all settled in without any problems at all. Leeds's Olivier Dacourt, another of my former team-mates in the under-20s, was also involved in that tournament in Japan, ensuring that the 'Frenchies' from the Premiership actually made up around half the national side!

The Confederations Cup merely confirmed that this France side was very sure of itself. Personally, I discovered a new position during the tournament, playing in a central midfield role alongside Patrick Vieira. I revelled in the new role; it was a bit like the role I'd played all those years before at Reims, or even at Marseille when Rolland Courbis had first asked me to take the game by the scruff of the neck. I'm not going to kid myself into believing I have the same qualities as Zinedine Zidane, but I can do a job when I've got the likes of Patrick and Eric Carrière at my side.

The new role brought extra responsibilities – at Arsenal I ask for them, with France I accept them when given – but I relished them and, to my enormous pride and surprise, the press voted me their player of the tournament. I scored against Brazil in our 2–1 semi-final success before we beat Japan 1–0 in the final. That was our third international trophy within three years. The fourth was supposed to be the World Cup in Japan and South Korea but, as we all now know, that wasn't to be.

Our failure at that tournament, as I've said, boiled down to two main factors: physical fatigue and mental exhaustion. In the future we must learn from the mistakes we made: like spending our time filming adverts rather than resting, fulfilling media duties when we should have had our feet up. Then, things will be different, and better. We have to ensure that when we run out at Euro 2004 we are ready for the challenge ahead.

Being picked for your country is special. The jersey with its blue, white and red bands represents our country; putting it on and hearing the first few notes of the _Marseillaise_ sends shivers down my spine. My attention remains fixed upon Euro 2004 and the World Cup in Germany two years later. Regardless of what I've already achieved in my career, and like any kid in France kicking a ball around in the streets, I still live for those moments and dream of being among _Les Bleus_.

7

Relaxation

I remember the night Arsenal hammered Bayer Leverkusen 4–1 in the Champions League. Such emphatic scorelines are rare at that level of football, especially when you're playing the Bundesliga leaders, but everything came off for us that evening. We had cohesion, creativity, precision and, above all, we took our chances. Highbury sang out in celebration.

That was one of the best atmospheres I've ever experienced in a stadium. The spectators were over the moon as five goals flew in and Thierry Henry and Patrick Vieira, two of our Frenchie scorers, ran the show. I also had a chance to score and duly netted our first.

At the end of the game, knackered but elated, I hurried to meet up with my wife and a friend of ours who was over for the match. Romane Bohringer, an actress (you could say she's the French equivalent of Sadie Frost), had come to London with her younger brother and was clearly quite taken by what she'd seen. 'Is it always like that here?' she asked after we'd embraced. Not every week, I told her, knowing that that type of atmosphere and near perfect performance only comes along once in a blue moon.

In reality, being a footballer is like being an actor. We are both delivering a performance, and the stadium is our theatre.

We often find ourselves on the road, in transit between games or training camps. I've come to know too well the airports of England, France and those across Europe. During these long hauls up and down the continent we not only have to keep ourselves busy to pass the time, we also have to prepare ourselves for the games. If you don't strike a balance between relaxation and preparation, you won't be ready to play the match.

I try to keep myself relaxed without ever forgetting that I'm part of a group. I'm a footballer, not a tennis player, and mine is a collective sport. I can't detach myself from the environment in which I'm playing. I know that Arsène Wenger is not a fan of players who don't like the collective side of the game, anyone who is too insular. Fortunately, I like the collective aspect of the game – all for one and one for all, harping back to my D'Artagnan nickname!

We occasionally fly between games in England, but our most frequent means of transport is the coach. The journeys are often quite long, but I consider time spent travelling on board as an opportunity to relax, even if my rule is never to let myself get caught up in a personal bubble, closed off from the outside world. That's why when it comes to music I won't use a Walkman; it's too much of a barrier.

I'm well aware that the up-and-coming match is the most important thing, and winning it is the thing to focus on, but I know I'll still have the period immediately before the game to think about that. So when I'm on the bus, I try to use the time to talk with my team-mates or have a laugh. Our conversations are about everything and anything – football, films, music . . . The most important thing is that this communication exists. I'll mainly talk to the other French players, given my limited command of English, but when I can't find the words with some of the local lads laughter usually fills in. And the common denominator is always music.

Once we get to the dressing room, that's the time to start really mentally preparing yourself for the game and try not to get too stressed out. Some players try to isolate themselves here, to sit on their own, either listening to the music or thinking about the match ahead, but they are very much in the minority. I just look at it as another opportunity to relax before kick-off. It's all about how you can concentrate best. I don't need to block out the noise around me to get mentally tuned; being relaxed does not mean your mind isn't concentrated on the job in hand. It's a matter of finding a balance between concentration and relaxation.

Changing rooms always tend to be in the bowels of the stadium and are charged with every kind of competitive emotion before, during and after a game, and it's there that the differences between the French and the English leagues really show themselves. In France, the players tend to see it as a place to be quiet and introspective. They concentrate their minds, contemplating the match ahead. In England, the dressing rooms erupt with boisterous noise. The players are dancing around and shouting almost right up to the start of the game itself. It's all just part of a process of psyching ourselves up, and I suppose an extension of the great tradition of park football in England. It's a good reminder that, despite all the money involved, we still should be doing this for fun.

That's what it's like at Arsenal: we prepare for a physical battle without asking ourselves questions, rather by confronting things head on. Even so, there's still a sense of serenity about the place. I've never seen Arsène looking nervous, and it's the same among the players. The only cries you hear are those accompanying the CDs played on the stereo. My personal preference is American rap music. Whether I'm in the car, on a plane or at home, I'll always have some Ja-Rul, Snoop Doggy Dog or J-Lo playing in the background. I remember hearing stories about Ian Wright before games, whipping the lads up and dancing as he played deafening music. That clearly brought him luck because he went on to score a record 185 goals for the club.

Every kick received and every injury suffered by the body is reflected in some way on your face, if only because physical work takes its toll as much on the soul as on the body.

At any given moment, if I feel off colour, whether mentally or physically, I'm open to any relaxation technique which can help me maintain my form or fitness. When my form was suffering at Marseille I started consulting a fasciatherapist based in Monaco. I felt as if there was too much pressure on my shoulders, and as a result my football had lost its way. It's the kind of alternative therapy that's still not that popular in English football, but attitudes are slowly changing with the arrival of foreign coaches and players who are much more open to this sort of thing.

My experience certainly helped me to recharge my confidence and rediscover the qualities in my game. The specialist spoke simply and directly during our short, to-the-point sessions, which never lasted more than an hour. It wasn't as if I would lie back on his couch while he treated me as a psychologist or psychoanalyst would a patient. He just asked me questions about what was worrying me and I would tell him about my performances with L'OM. He concentrated his attentions on my face, and by analysing how I reacted he knew exactly which part of my body was tense and would massage my head to free me up so that I might feel more relaxed. During my last five months at Marseille, that therapy really helped me. I could feel the results of the treatment almost immediately and my game improved drastically. I haven't consulted the therapist since, but I'll always remain open to alternative therapies such as this.

A treatment I've yet to try is yoga. My wife suggested I give it a go, thinking it would complement the other relaxation techniques I already use, but what with all my club commitments I haven't had time to explore it.

To heal properly after an injury, and to prepare oneself for the next match, it's imperative that you take time to recuperate properly. There's so much physical contact in football that the muscles in the legs in particular are very susceptible as they're forever taking the strain. The day after a game we all meet up at London Colney for a warm-down session. There are a lot of stretches and leisurely jogs, all aimed at getting rid of the toxins and lactic acid that have built up in the body after the physical effort of the day before. After that I'll usually go for a swim in the pool at the training complex. Swimming gives me a real sense of well-being. The fact that Arsenal have a pool is a major plus; it distinguishes them from a lot of other clubs that don't have that kind of infrastructure. Clubs in France are usually well equipped, but at Arsenal the players have the means to prepare themselves in the best possible environment with top-of-the-range equipment and facilities.

It always comes back to this notion of equilibrium. You can easily spot a well-balanced athlete – there's harmony, almost elegance, in his movements. Two of my favourite sportsmen demonstrate this exactly: the Spanish footballer Michel and the tennis player Pete Sampras. Michel had that classiness associated with all the greats. To stay at the top in a sport like tennis where the world number one should change quite frequently is proof of Sampras's talent, but also of his desire to pay attention to the minutest detail. Both Michel and Sampras make it all look so simple and, perhaps as a result, play on the public's emotions. They're not perfect, no one is, but they are as close as you can get and their results speak for themselves.

Of course, there is someone else whose role is crucial in my preparation for games: my wife Nathalie. She has to cope with me when things aren't going well out on the pitch, or in the treatment room, and she helps me keep my confidence up. On the flipside, if I'm playing well and the rave reviews are coming, she keeps my feet on the ground. I can rely on her 100 per cent. If she's not happy, though, I feel it too. When we first came to London she found it hard to adapt not only to the English weather, but also to the mentality and new surroundings. The fact that she could speak the language did at least help. But she's made new friends now and has settled in well. I couldn't have done it without her.

All year round I find myself engrossed in football 24–7. Life is a constant cycle of training, going to games, playing and training again, so sometimes I have to just escape completely from that round ball or I'd go mad. A bit of variety can't be bad when you're preparing to compete at the top level.

My big thing is go-carting. It really takes my mind off things. When I was at Olympique de Marseille I used to organise several sessions for my team-mates down at the carting track. Zooming around in one of those things requires a different kind of concentration. Some of my team-mates, like Frank Leboeuf, prefer to play golf to relax; I'd much rather cart! It's the speed, the risk, the competition

. . . I haven't been able to go carting since coming to Arsenal, but it's still one of my favourite hobbies, and I plan to check out the north London opportunities soon.

When we're on the road, especially with the French team, we also tend to play a lot of cards. We've started doing the same at Arsenal recently too. I like the team spirit that's created by cards – the more people involved the better, increasing the competition and, of course, the cheating! That's a laugh.

But carting and cards are more winter activities. In summer, I really escape from football by getting away and travelling. I returned to Portugal after Euro 2000, going back to my family's roots, but I have two other destinations I love to visit. I'm forever lured south to the Mediterranean, and with Nathalie I always spend some of my summer holidays on Corsica. I love the tranquillity down there; plenty of other players holiday on the island too, people I've played against in the French league and former team-mates like Eric Roy. They've become my friends now.

Further south still is Morocco. I go there whenever I can in search of sun and sand. I stay at the La Mamounia hotel, but the people interest me as much as the country. I love listening to Hassan Kachloul and Mustapha Hadji, the Moroccans at Aston Villa, talking about their country; Hassan talks about Marrakesh, where he comes from, and Mousse of the desert he loves. I've also spoken to Abdelatif Benazzi, the rugby player at Saracens who was born in Oujda. When he talks about that part of the world it's fascinating. I listen to my Moroccan friends talking about 'their' Morocco and find myself thinking about 'my' Ponte de Lima, my holidays in Oviedo and my memories of Reims.

A footballer's mental world is structured by his coaches, trainers and team-mates, but also by his close circle of friends and family. Those people can help you experience things you might not otherwise touch. I finished school at 17 years old, and at the time I preferred to strut around Reims town centre or play football rather than read. I've always liked the cinema, too, and my favourite actors are Al Pacino, Robert de Niro and Jack Nicholson. The advertising campaigns I front are as close to acting as I'm ever likely to get. You realise then what's needed to pull it off; you have to pay attention to the smallest detail, the best light, the best angle and so on. The first take is fine, but the second, third, fourth . . . With each shot you have to take into account myriad tiny differences. Doing the same take 15 times in a row can try your patience.

Recently, on my wife's suggestion, I've discovered the theatre. As I've said, Nathalie had met and become friends with Romane Bohringer by chance on a skiing holiday. They got on really well, and Romane invited Nathalie to one of her performances. She was going to be on the stage in a small production in a Paris suburb, a Shakespearean play, in French no less! Romane, who was playing two roles, that of a queen who dies and then that of her daughter, invited us both to go along and Nathalie promised her that she'd try to convince me to come. I was in Paris and free that weekend towards the end of the

2001/02 season. That night PSG were playing Marseille at
Parc des Princes, leaving me with a choice of going to the
football in the posh 16th *arrondissement* or to Shakespeare
out in the suburbs! Admittedly under pressure from
Nathalie, I opted for the theatre; for the first time in my life
I was going to sit through a play. The performance lasted
three hours but I hardly noticed the time passing. I found
the experience a totally mind-expanding one. Romane was
great and the story seemed to be entirely contemporary,
almost like a soap opera.

Increasingly I can see why my former under-20s coach
Raymond Domenech, an ex-player and an amateur actor
himself, kept saying going to the theatre would be an
excellent pastime for us all to take up. Footballers prepare
themselves like actors before they go out on stage. We dress,
for instance, put on our kit just like actors change into their
costumes. From the dressing rooms or changing rooms, we
both wait and listen to the noise from the terraces (or stalls)
before making our entrance. We may not have a curtain like
they do in the theatre, but we have a tunnel which serves
much the same function, and we both emerge under the
spotlights. Once we're underway, the disciplines needed for
acting are much the same as those needed to play football,
particularly when it comes to concentration. We have to be
precise with each movement, they have to be the same with
each word they speak. They, like us, play out their roles in
front of an expectant audience. The public are their critics,
and whether you are accepted or not, and therefore progress
or not, is largely down to them.

I'm afraid to say I'd lost that build-up, that thrill of the performance, in France. In England, football is very much a show and anyone prepared to give it a go and show off their skills is applauded. In the Premiership, even if some of the fancy tricks or flips don't come off, the fans appreciate what you're trying to do and applaud anyway. When people come to a stadium, they want to see a good game whatever the result. If not, why would the likes of Arsène Wenger and Patrick Vieira still be managing and playing in England? Over here the custom is for the players to applaud the fans who have been encouraging them to win at the end of the game. The next time Romane comes to Highbury or I go and see one of her plays, we'll better understand the similarities in our lines of work. In the sixteenth century the audience in any theatre played an interactive part in the proceedings, shouting out and talking to the actors on stage. Isn't that exactly the same relationship those on the terraces enjoy with footballers these days? Loads of fans cheer or boo us out on the pitch. I like that analogy between Shakespearean theatre and the Premiership. Never mind football being the new religion, I reckon it's the new Shakespeare.

When I was playing in France I'd watch the English game without appreciating how important a part the fans played. Now I'm here I understand how it all works so much better. The fans may be up on the terraces, but they're no more than five metres at most from the players. Knowing they're there to help you and encourage you tends to give you wings, except of course when you're surrounded by the opposing fans. I'm sure this close proximity with the supporters helped me adapt to English football when I first arrived at Arsenal. The supporters were very generous to me from the start.

During the season we don't have much time to spend on our hobbies, mainly because between competitive games and recuperation we often have to fit in media duties. I was contacted at the start of the 2001/02 season by a French radio station, Europe 1, to host a half-hour slot on their show *Europ'sport*. I had to give it some thought; would I talk to the listeners about my passions outside football, or talk in detail about the game itself? I accepted the invitation mainly because I wanted to experience something new, to work in a different environment to football, and I feel that generally my relationship with the media is good. Sure, I have had a few run-ins with some people, particularly during my time at Marseille, but that taught me plenty. I understand now that an article is a means of expression. As long as the newspapers (or other media) analyse my game and not my private life, then that's fine. I can take criticism. It just spurs me on.

The radio slot, which is called 'Club Pires', was to run on Thursday evenings when there are no European or domestic games taking place. The station set up a little studio in my home in London so I can host it from there each week, but the whole experience of talking with a couple of guests gives me an opportunity to do what I like most: to communicate. Just as I love talking with my team-mates at the team hotel, on the coach or in the changing rooms before or after a game, I appreciate listening to others who have something to ask or to tell me.

I choose one of my weekly guests but the other is down to Europe 1, ensuring that I meet and talk with new people each week. One of the first people to take part was Pascal Obispo. I was one of the people he involved when recording a record to raise money for research into AIDS. Other footballers took part in that as well, like Marcel Desailly, who also later appeared on the show. I like the idea of the worlds of football and music coming together to raise money for a cause like that.

On Europe 1 we also interviewed Raphaël Ibanez, the former captain of the French rugby team. I know a bit about that sport thanks to my friendship with Thomas Castaignède – rugby allies courage, determination, finesse and intelligence in a single sport. We also talked with Sébastien Amiez, the slalom skier from Pralognan-la-Vanoise, silver medallist at Salt Lake City and winner a few years back of the World Cup downhill title. Sportsmen know how to talk to each other; Sébastien had also been sidelined by serious injury and had also tasted victory at international level. During our conversation we discovered plenty of things we had in common. I also had other footballers on the show, people I'd come across during my career, including Pierre-Yves André, with whom I'd played for the under-20s, and David Terrier, my team-mate from Metz. Each one had his own stories and had experienced different aspects of life in the game, but we always gave the impression that we were coming from the same place. We also had Carlo Molinari, my former chairman at Metz, who recalled my good times wearing the maroon shirt. Even so, and as much as I enjoyed the work, I've still got a good few years in me yet before I turn into a full-time disc jockey!

I've already put France's failure at the World Cup down to the players being tired after doing too much in the build-up to the tournament, but I would say that, if I'd been fit enough to go to Japan, my radio show with Europe 1 barely ate into my everyday life. The broadcasts were done from my front room with me sitting in my favourite armchair and would only take half an hour out of my day, hardly enough to leave me mentally exhausted.

I love radio. I feel much more at ease doing that than being on television – that doesn't interest me at all right now. I'm really up for communicating with people, with a microphone in my hand. On radio, you listen to people and respond, whereas television is more about cultivating an image. Europe 1 gave me a chance not only to try my hand at a different job, but also to experience my wife's work – she's got a slot as a presenter on the famous Laurent Ruquier's show on the same channel. I get good vibes from being on the radio, different to those I get when I go carting or to the theatre. I'd say I'm as relaxed there as I would be sitting by a Corsican creek or lying on a Moroccan beach.

I often think about the different paths that may open up for me in the future. The media plays a major role in our lives as professional sportsmen, just as it does in society in general. As long as I'm able to express myself and I'm my own boss, that's fine. Maybe I'll end up doing that. I'll just follow my instinct – that same voice inside my head that told me to become a footballer all those years ago.

I'm 29. I reckon I've still got five years of football ahead of me at the top level and my objective has to be to compete in the World Cup in Germany in 2006. Maybe that cut-off at the age of 33 could be extended. We'll see what physical state I'm in over the next few seasons with my club and country. I'd like to stop playing as late as possible, to play right up until the moment when my body tells me it can't take it any more. That just shows how passionately I love this job. The joy it brings me makes me want to keep playing as long as I can.

But when the times comes to hang up my boots, I don't envisage staying in professional football. To become a trainer or manager you need a certain charisma, to know how to throw your voice. It's not in my nature, as my spell as captain of Marseille showed me. Shouting, haranguing and slagging the players isn't really me, so I don't see myself sitting on the bench issuing tactical orders or yelling at the lads. On the other hand, I wouldn't rule out working in amateur football, perhaps coaching youngsters of 15 or 16. At that impressionable age, when some youngsters slip through the system for a variety of reasons, guidance is needed most of all. I'd like to help them make it in this job. Perhaps I'll go back to Sainte-Anne and coach the kids at the club where it all started for me, give something back.

It's true that I was only recognised quite late on, when I

was 25 years old, but I still feel as if my career has followed the right course. All the hard work appears to have paid off. And anyway, making people sit up when you're young, say at 20, isn't always ideal. The most important thing is doing what you love and enjoying it, and that's what happened in my case. My career has only become more 'noticed' since I came to play in a foreign country at Arsenal where games are televised around the globe, but every move I've made, from Reims to Metz to Marseille to London, has been for sporting reasons.

Whether I'm playing for Arsenal or France, I think I've got the same outlook on the game these days as when I was playing at Metz as a young professional. The difference is that nowadays I take more risks with my game. That's thanks to Arsène Wenger, and it made celebrating the Double with Arsenal, even with my knee bandaged and crutches at my side, all the more satisfying.

I was desperate to get back to fitness and pull on that number seven shirt again. If there's one superstition I do have, it's for the number seven. If I play cards, I don't care if my hand is stacked with spades or clubs as long as I have a seven. It's my lucky number. When I came to Arsenal the first thing I told the vice-chairman David Dein was, 'I'll come and play for you if you give me the number seven shirt.' I didn't start by asking for money or talking about the length of the contract on the table, but about my shirt number. I've worn the number seven throughout my career and it's always brought me luck. When Didier Deschamps retired from international football I went to see him and said, 'Dédé, congratulations on a magnificent career. But, now that's out of the way, I'm having your number!' He just looked at me with a smile. 'If it's you who takes up the number seven,' he said, 'then all the better.' I hope I have justified that reaction.

Football has provided me with an education in life. Within the game I have learned how to respect rules, how to work and how to persevere to achieve what I want. The sport is all about team spirit, letting people work together towards a common goal. Much is made of football dividing people, but it unites them as well – look at France after the World Cup success in 1998, or even the Arsenal supporters after our Double in 2002. Here, in a foreign country, I have been welcomed and accepted as one of their own. That is why I chose this career. *Footballeur.*